UNMUTE YOUR *Heart*

A Voice of Victory
Overcoming Domestic Abuse

Second Edition

by Sharon R. Wynn

Christian Living Books, Inc.
Largo, MD

Copyright © 2019 Sharon R. Wynn

All rights reserved under the international copyright law. No part of this book may be reproduced or transmitted in any form or by any means, electronic or mechanical, including photocopying, recording, or by any information storage and retrieval system, without the express, written permission of the publisher or the author. The exception is reviewers, who may quote brief passages in a review.

ISBN 9781562293581

Christian Living Books, Inc.
P. O. Box 7584
Largo, MD 20792
christianlivingbooks.com
We bring your dreams to fruition.

Unless otherwise noted, Scripture quotations are taken from the King James Version of the Bible.

Scripture quotations marked NKJV are taken from the New King James Version®. Copyright © 1982 by Thomas Nelson. Used by permission. All rights reserved.

Printed in the United States of America.

Library of Congress Cataloging-in-Publication Data

Names: Wynn, Sharon R., 1972- author.
Title: Unmute your heart : a voice of victory overcoming domestic abuse / by Sharon R. Wynn.
Description: Second edition. | Largo, MD : Christian Living Books, Inc., [2019] | Includes bibliographical references and index. | Summary: "Discusses domestic abuse by her husband, a former NFL player and pastor, and how survivors can overcome abuse"-- Provided by publisher.
Identifiers: LCCN 2019019489 (print) | LCCN 2019980715 (ebook) | ISBN 9781562293581 (paperback) | ISBN 9781562293659 (ebook)
Subjects: LCSH: Wynn, Sharon R., 1972- | Christian biography--United States. | Abused wives--United States--Biography. | Wife abuse--Religious aspects--Christianity.
Classification: LCC BR1725.W96 A3 2019 (print) | LCC BR1725.W96 (ebook) | DDC 261.8/327092 [B]--dc23
LC record available at https://lccn.loc.gov/2019019489
LC ebook record available at https://lccn.loc.gov/2019980715

DEDICATION

First and foremost, I dedicate this book to God for inspiring me to write about my journey through domestic abuse and a subsequent bitter divorce. I appreciate my Lord and Savior for guiding and keeping me in perfect peace as I fixed my mind on Him.

CONTENTS

Foreword vii

Introduction 11

Chapter 1 – My Reality 15

Chapter 2 – The Process 29

Chapter 3 – Fruit of the Spirit 41

Chapter 4 – Barbie Doll 51

Chapter 5 – Unmute Your Heart 59

Chapter 6 – Can You Hear Me Now? 65

Chapter 7 – The Star 71

Chapter 8 – Caught in The Cross Fire 79

Chapter 9 – Seasons 87

Chapter 10 – Living to Speak and Declare 93

Chapter 11 – My Secret 99

Chapter 12 – My Children 105

Other Works by the Author 111

Acknowledgments 113

About the Author 115

FOREWORD

Sharon Wynn's pivotal memoir is not long in number of pages but is powerful in depth of thought. It's a very moving sharing of the struggles and challenges of a failed marriage. What she went through could have permanently destroyed her mental, emotional and physical health if not for learning to overcome the trails of life by walking closer with God.

It's not an easy task to share personal and sometimes painful experiences without exposing a little of your own frailties and deficiencies. But the humility that she exhibits clearly illustrates her desire to help others through similar situations. She shows others how they too can persevere through the storms of life even though it may not appear that a positive outcome is possible.

How do we personally and individually respond to emotional pain and suffering? How do we move forward with our lives after experiencing psychological trauma that leaves emotional scars? How do we manage anxiety, resentment and anger without it consuming us and causing mental and or physical illness? Allowing these emotions to remain in your spirit will mute your heart.

Sharon's Barbie Doll who "is lifeless but looks full of life" is an excellent analogy of women who lack fulfillment and happiness in their lives but externally radiate a false impression to others.

Sharon's journey through a broken relationship resulted in divorce. But she gives a lot of insight into how women can rebuild their lives by letting go and "letting the Word of God be activated in to receive the manifestation of their healing."

Unmute Your Heart is a very good book and a book that I plan to in my practice.

–Kirk Brocks, PsyD
LMFT, Private Practice

Therapy is an interesting phenomenon that takes place between the client and their therapist. As the therapist and client build their rapport. At times the client is not always ready to talk about their issues. So, the therapist will start with unconditionally positive regard in a non-threatening environment that will ensure the establishment of a nonjudgmental and a trusting environment.

As the therapist probes the client and asks questions such as *What brings you here? How long have you been experiencing these symptoms? How does this effect you?* The client may struggle intrapsychically (within the mind or personality) with anguish as they negotiate within themselves how much of their life story and history that they would like to share. The negotiation is entangled with self-esteem, judging self, family history, taboos, and fears. Sometimes it takes years before the client reveals – or come to their own understanding about – the root of a problem because of the mask they have worn to protect themselves.

Trauma is like an onion; the more layers you shed the more layers are exposed. Sharon Wynn has strategically placed us in a safe environment that allows us to see and experience her process of becoming a conqueror. Sharon's transparency allows us to witness her vulnerability as she is simultaneously being transformed by God's love.

The term *adversarial growth* is a concept in resiliency that highlights adversity and propels people to function at higher levels after experiencing a life changing event. Adversarial circumstances create opportunities to springboard into greater awareness and insight that redefines our purpose and meaning in life.

> And we know that all things work together for good to them that love God, to them who are the called according to his purpose. (Romans 8:28)

Church hurt can be devastating and have lasting impact. Occupying church titles does not preclude you from experiencing pain. Whether you are a parishioner or a first lady, the in-depth analysis of Sharon's process will encourage you to trust God, face your issues, learn, grow, and hold on despite the pain you have or are experiencing. So unmute your heart and allow God to turn your tears into triumph and your pain into purpose.

–Norris DuPree, Jr., Ph.D.
MFT, Psychologist, LADC

INTRODUCTION

Many of us may have shared some of the same joys, losses, pains, hurts, fears or accomplishments. We have also overcome many challenges while pushing forward as works-in-progress to be better in every aspect of life.

You may have encountered severe challenges that caused you to mute your heart and change as a woman. Maybe you were the loving type, but hurt and rejection have made you angry, guarded, and cold. Maybe you were the trusting type, but unfaithfulness, deceit, and lies have made you bitter, frustrated, and skeptical of everyone and everything. Granted, being human, you may have experienced different types of emotions because of what you encountered. However, the most important thing we must all do to move forward is to unmute our hearts.

So how do we unmute our hearts you ask? Determination, faith, and hard work will produce a heart of forgiveness that can release the most damaging toxic emotions that block you from moving forward into your future. You must confront exposed or hidden issues, so you can open the gateway to your destiny and purpose.

Do you want to change your perspective or outlook on your life? Then see yourself beyond your process. Your process is something you must go through. It will shape you into who you were made to be. This takes work, courage, and strength because you must develop your relationship with God through the mind of Christ, which is His Word. Depending on the severity of the trauma you experienced, professional, godly counsel will help you through your healing process mentally and emotionally. I am a witness that these components can see us through many hurtful events; they helped to usher me into a healthier and more rewarding place in my life.

The battle is not ours; it belongs to God. Through prayer, we can continue to fight for what is worth fighting for. That is our joy, peace, love, happiness, and the essence of who we are. My friends, you are fearfully and wonderfully made. You are even better when you choose to unmute your hearts.

UNMUTE YOUR *Heart* WORKBOOK

Survival Kit Tools for Overcoming Domestic Abuse

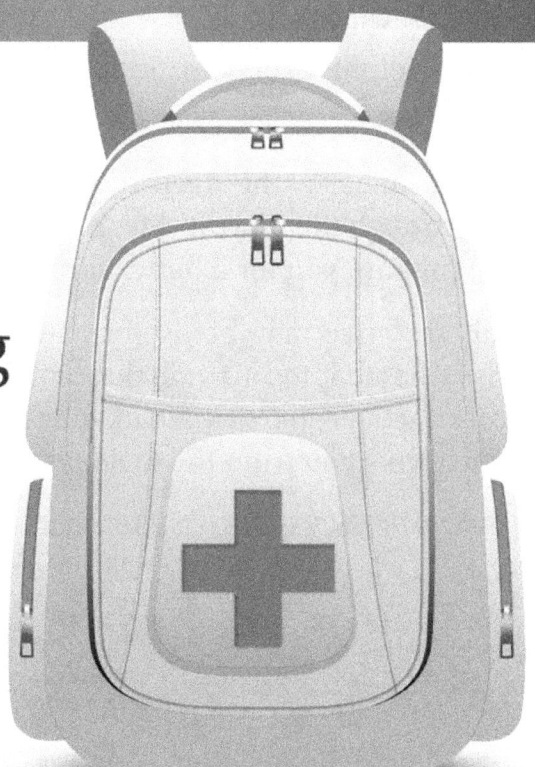

SHARON R. WYNN

What's in Your Survival Kit?

Find the courage to survive the horrors of abuse and divorce by applying the practical steps in this workbook, the companion to *Unmute Your Heart*.

The survival kit is well-designed to help you get to the heart of the matter. Its spiritual truths, practical exercises, and tough questions will aid you in honestly examining your feelings, shining the light of God on the difficult issues, and moving forward. Inside each kit you will find...

- Food for Thought
- Key Truths
- Thought Provoking Challenges and Questions
- Backpack Tools
- Helpful Exercises, Scriptures and Prayers
- Resources for Abuse Survivors

As you unearth the deep-rooted fears, insecurities, soul ties, and strongholds in your life, the process may be painful, but it will prepare you for a better future.

This resource may be used by individuals or groups and can easily be adapted to suit the requirements for either. Do the work! Actively participate in your healing and recovery as God transforms you from the inside out.

ISBN   9781562293642 | 8.5" x 11" | Paperback | 76 pages
Available wherever books are sold or from ChristianLivingBooks.com

CHAPTER 4

MY REALITY

As we go through life, we become accustomed to everything as we see it – the people we live with, our church families, and our loved ones. We become very comfortable with the familiar, so when life suddenly changes, we are left stranded at the crossroads desperately trying to figure out which way to go.

That's exactly what happened to me when my ex filed for a divorce and walked out on me and our children. Much later, he claimed that he did it to get my attention. He was obsessed with thoughts of me not wanting or loving him because I was blossoming into a young woman. He could not break free from the strongholds of that mindset. It was his reality.

Though he frequently threatened to divorce me, in order to maintain control, I never imagined coming home and finding him gone. His closet was empty, except for the hangers, a sock here, a shoe there, and a few garments left behind on the floor. They served as absolute reminders that he was once a part of my life and had now vanished. He was gone forever. I was afraid because this time, it felt different.

I could feel my heart pounding in my chest and a lump in my throat as I swallowed. I stood there speechless looking into his closet.

I felt the woman who had suppressed the strength and courage inside her for years begin to wake up and transform. I hid my strength and courage for so long I thought they were not there anymore. But in some supernatural way, God empowered me again. He would not let me fall apart. Immediately, I reminded myself I had five children who needed me. I had to be strong for them and needed to make sound decisions as to how I was going to provide and take care of them.

Questions flooded my mind. *Is this for real? Is this temporary? What is this?* It deconstructed so much of what I believed was my reality. My world came crumbling down. I felt as though I had lost everything, and I was buried under the rubble of what was left behind.

The valuable, priceless, precious things I held so dear could no longer be found. Everything I thought I knew, the home and the people close to me whom I called my neighbors, were nowhere to be found. The friends who visited the very place I called home would no longer come because that familiar place was destroyed; everything was gone. I was so lost, not even a map could lead anyone to me.

How would I survive this one? How would I face the shame now that everything was exposed? Everybody would see and know what truly took place in our home.

I went on a journey and realized I had no control over my circumstances. I was forced to accept the hand I was dealt. I could choose to remain at the crossroads or move ahead despite the challenges.

I had to deal with the untruths he told and the gossip brewing in the church we both pastored and loved so much. I had to battle within me to hold my head high and pull my shoulders back for the sake of my children and our future.

Chapter 1 ■ My Reality

My children were young, so, thoughts of the damage done frightened me. I was petrified to even think about the impact it would have on *their* lives. At times, their actions showed signs of the scars and the bruises that were left behind, but I prayed and stood on the Word of God for complete healing, restoration, and deliverance for my entire family.

SO MANY SACRIFICES

I would often ask, *Why did he leave us? What did I do wrong?* I felt like I had given my all. Even when I should have spoken up for myself, I didn't, because the reality was I. Could. Not!

All of the sacrifices that I made within the 20 years of our marriage all seemed to amount to nothing. I prayed for him and supported him as he was trying to fulfill his dream of becoming an NFL player, which he eventually did.

> *I was so lost, not even a map could lead anyone to me.*

After the last college game of the season he suffered a severe ankle injury. He was devastated because he felt that this injury would cause him to miss out in the NFL draft. He would no longer be a top pick player making the big bucks. The road ahead was going to be more challenging than I anticipated.

He was eventually drafted in the 12th round by the Los Angeles Rams. But when his injury forced him out of training camp that summer he was cut from the team. In less than three weeks he was sent home with his last check that would have to last us for a while until he could find another job to continue to pay our bills.

Months after being cut he had his first surgery, but he was anxious to stay in shape and wanted to get back on the field to pursue his dream. He ate, slept and drank football. This went on for years.

There I was loving, supporting and cheering him on as a good wife would do, right? Every two years it seemed we were moving here or there. I was having babies and became frustrated because I just wanted to be settled and have a normal family life. All in all, I was in it for better or worse, for richer or poorer. We lived with his aunt, his mother, my mother, my sister and again with my mother. All throughout those phases of our lives I remained supportive and even took care of him again after the second surgery on his ankle. All the while he was still determined to reach his goal.

When he got picked up by the San Francisco 49ers things went well for a while. However, he was still not healthy enough to remain on the team and was cut over 3 or 4 times because of his ankle. Once he got better, he signed on with the Canadian Football League, then the World League of American Football and finally, the Oakland Raiders. He was cut from the Raiders in the late nineties.

I had gone along for the ride, but was glad that when it was finally over because maybe now we could settle ourselves. He battled a lot of frustration and lack of fulfillment since he did not really accomplish things the way he wanted to. I was there for him in spite of it all. There is a lot of pressure and stress when trying to compete for a job against big name football players making the big bucks. It was hard for him, since a spot on the team was not guaranteed from week to week. This made things very tense in the home. Everything was exacerbated by the fact that he was in constant pain and I supported him because I was ride or die.

I was finally able to get back into school and pursue my education in early childhood development. When I opened up a childcare business, God blessed us to finally be settled. This allowed me to bring in a healthy, stable income and purchase our first home. I yet covered for him by purposefully making him feel adequate and as though he was still the sole provider in our household. The funny thing is that people automatically assumed that everything that the business enabled us to acquire was due to the residuals from his football career. I allowed them to think that, but they had no idea of the suffering, homelessness and lack we endured.

I was a good wife and mother and for everything to play out the way that it did was beyond hurtful. I gave everything. Divorce was never even in my vocabulary. I was totally committed to my marriage and my family. Yet, years later he turned his back and walked out on me and our children.

The nagging thoughts of disappointment and betrayal still pick at me. When they do, I have to reflect and realize that I am still blessed. I have to constantly rebuke and silence every negative word from the Enemy. I have to remind myself that I can make it if I stay focused and prayerfully move forward. I have to maintain the confidence in knowing that God will never leave me nor forsake me.

Living my new reality has not been easy at all. However, it has birthed new life and new opportunities for me to encourage others to never quit and never give in. Through the heat and pressure of our pain we will emerge as beautiful as diamonds.

KEEP MOVING FORWARD

No matter how devastating your storm is life still goes on. The clock keeps on ticking and waits for no one. You must fight and never stop moving forward!

I remember lying down to take a nap, bothered by the events taking place in my life. I was somewhat asleep and somewhat awake when I had the following epiphany:

"Where are we going, Mommy?" I heard one of my children say.

"Come on," I replied. "God will provide."

We noticed every other home in our neighborhood was still standing. The happy sounds of children outside laughing and playing could be heard. The smell of dinner cooking on the stove filled the air. It was a beautiful day; the sun was shining, and there was not a cloud in sight. But I felt confused because life continued around me. How could these people go on with their lives when mine had stopped?

As we walked down the street, I felt lost, helpless, and embarrassed. In the distance, I heard someone say, "Hello, First Lady! How are you doing?"

I thought to myself, "Don't they understand what has happened?" I know they saw my home flat on the ground. Didn't that concern them? Yet, in the midst of my confusion, I had a sudden perception that they needed to keep their lives as normal as possible because they still loved the ministry at our church.

The people at the church saw the devastation, but few of them felt it. However, it was not their problem. They needed to stay neutral. Some said hello, while others didn't. Some picked a side and ignored me, while others didn't. Some people simply chose to move on and continue with their lives.

I understood the dynamics that were at play and accepted that's just the way it is. I decided to work on me. After all, I have a story to tell. I am a survivor! Therefore, I need to let others know that life will deal you a hand, but it's up to you to play and win or give up and lose. I chose to play and win.

AN UNEXPECTED JOURNEY

During this time, I had to reach within myself and see what I was really made of. I began to understand how much I trusted and depended on my ex but not enough on God. We got married at a very young age. He was the only man I had ever known. I looked to him to fill the voids that I now understand only God can truly fill. This led me on an unexpected journey to develop a closer relationship with God.

Growing up in church, I would always hear testimonies of everybody else's encounters with God. People would talk about how He opened doors, healed the sick, and made ways out of no way. He was a friend to the friendless and a mother to the motherless. Quite frankly, even though I believed all that, I could not identify with what they were saying. I never experienced it in *my* life. However, at the same time, unbeknownst to me, I was going through situations that were designed to strengthen and teach me valuable life lessons. They would equip me to conquer what was to come and give me a bold testimony that I could share about what *my* God can do.

A songwriter said, "It is no secret what God can do. What He's done for others, He'll do for you." This is where I began to develop my relationship with God through prayer and reading His Word. I got to experience Who He is for myself. Even though I felt like I couldn't make it on my own, I could with the help of the Lord. He has watched over me and my children and made provisions for us through the years. He has never let me down.

MANIFESTING GREATNESS

God began to build my confidence in areas where I felt weak. Consequently, I developed a desire to strengthen and encourage others. I never considered myself to be a writer, but one day at work in 2011, shortly after my divorce was final, I started writing. It was a bittersweet journey. I would pick it up and put it down, but all the while, I was experiencing many hurtful events that would reveal the purpose of my assignment. The journey was necessary for me to help many others, and it pushed me to birth this book. I purchased a laptop, and the rest is history.

I encourage you to do the impossible things. Don't stop believing God until you see His promises manifested in your life. I always knew there was greatness in me, and so did others. However, I had to transition from knowing there was greatness in me to manifesting the greatness in me.

One of the hardest things for me to accept is that many of our painful experiences are simply meant to help somebody else. I really had to ask myself why I would want to help someone when I had to endure something so hurtful. I wondered, why couldn't God fix what was broken? It seemed very unfair.

God began to comfort my heart and teach me to see things from another angle. He showed me that He can get the glory and the victory out of every circumstance. He is the Comforter and mender of my broken heart. What I discovered was that every time He blessed me with an opportunity to share my testimony or words of encouragement with hurting men and women, I would feel a sense of joy and fulfillment. I had the comfort of knowing that everything I had gone through was not wasted.

A PRAYING MOTHER

My mother is an awesome woman of God. I have watched her life. She and my father raised nine children, and she remained with my dad until God called him home. She is a prayer warrior. A lot of what I learned was simply part of my process, but I thank God that through her life, I had a great point of reference for a wife, mother, and First Lady.

My mother is like a chess player, never making a move without consulting the heavenly Father. She sought His counsel to ensure every move she made was the right one. When God said, "Move," she moved. When God said, "Go," she went. Every step of the way I have seen God make provisions for her. Hence, I have learned that if you follow God, He will usher you into your destiny.

I've observed the way my mother labors in prayer and stays in fellowship with God. I remember when my two younger daughters and I went to stay with my mother for a while after my divorce. She would wake me up at five in the morning to pray. I was so broken, I didn't even know the words to say, but I knew that the prayers would favorably impact my life.

> Confess your faults one to another, and pray one for another, that ye may be healed. The effectual fervent prayer of a righteous man availeth much. (James 5:16)

I know God honors my mother's prayers because of the life she lives. I am so grateful for what she and my father instilled in all their children.

My mother is a class act. She looks beautiful every day no matter what she is going through or where she is going; she is an excellent example to her family. Through difficult times, she stayed busy being constructive and focused on her goals and purpose. Her actions taught me that even though we go through fiery trials, we don't stop; we don't quit. Instead, we keep it moving because tomorrow is coming, and it's going to be a brighter day. So, stick around to see and enjoy it.

We must also be mindful of how we go through trials because people are watching. Some are for you, and yes, some are against you. However, if God is for you, He is more than the world against you.

TRUST THE PROCESS

I learned the art of patience through my reality. When you are used to being intimate and sharing your life with someone, it is a shock to your system when they are gone. The loss of even the seemingly insignificant things can be painful. Your nights can be quiet and lonely. You long for the intimacy you were used to having. That desire for closeness may overshadow the truth about what the relationship was really like.

Throughout that period, remember your value and worth. You want something meaningful and fulfilling. This is the time to get in touch with yourself, so you can improve *you*. Rehearse the promises of God and live in expectation of them. In other words, look for each promise to be fulfilled. Fall in love with Jesus all over again, and rededicate your life to Him. Also, make good on the things you promised Him.

Develop yourself in the Word and in prayer. Remain faithful to God. Be an asset, not a liability. Even when you feel like your life is in shambles and you can't do anything about it, stop complaining about everything. If you delight yourself in God, let go, and let Him work. He will give you the desires of your heart.

There's no need to lash out, retaliate, and seek to hurt others because you are hurt. Become a better you! Your reward is your success. We are here with a purpose. Remember, most of what we experience is to help somebody else. I purposed in my heart that I will be for someone what *I* needed someone to be for me during the most challenging times of my life. It took some time to embrace that, but I did.

You're not alone even though you may feel you are. You just have to trust the process. Don't rush it! When we rush the process, we leave the will of God. Believe you me, when God has a purpose for you, He will let you try things your way because He gives us free will. But you can prolong getting to your destiny with the unnecessary choices you make. Praise God, He has a way of getting you back on track.

SELF-REFLECTION

Find out who you are.
- What makes you happy?
- What makes you sad?
- What are your likes and dislikes?
- Do you like you?

- Do you care about yourself?
- Do you have respect for yourself?
- How is work?
- How is home?
- How is your family?

There are so many questions to ask about the things that matter to you. It is equally important to find the answers.

You are growing older like a good, aged wine waiting to be used for a special occasion. You're not cheap at all. In fact, even a little bit of the precious time you give to any man makes him wealthy. *So how should a man handle you?* Very carefully. He should engage you with excitement, anticipation, and respect. He should love, hold, embrace, and savor you, your hair, skin, eyes – everything that makes you a beautiful woman in full bloom. You can't be wasted on foolishness!

THE ALABASTER BOX

Each of the four gospels recounts the story of Mary pouring a precious and priceless ointment on Jesus:

> Then she broke the [alabaster] flask and poured it on [Jesus] head. But there were some who were indignant among themselves, and said, "Why was this fragrant oil wasted?" But Jesus said, "Let her alone. Why do you trouble her? She has done a good work for Me. She has done what she could." Wherever this gospel is preached in the whole world, what this woman has done will also be told as a memorial to her." (Mark 14:4, 6, 8, 9 NKJV)

Only a true love can treasure and know what's inside your alabaster box. Guard it within your heart. Mary believed that Jesus was worthy to receive the treasure in the alabaster box. The box was only broken on rare and special occasions.

What happens when the man you're with suddenly becomes aware of your beauty and pricelessness? What do you do when he is actually afraid of losing you, a rare gift? After all, to him, the transformation seems to have taken place overnight. Why? Because he stopped, looked, and finally took notice of you after several years – as my ex did.

I would like to call that transition a turning of the tides. Everything changes; nothing remains the same. This is really a wonderful time for a husband and wife to explore, discover, and fulfill your exotic desires with each other. As two lovers, this should heighten your passion for each other. Rekindle and ignite the flames of yesterday. Set your love life on fire to burn up those displeasing feelings of loneliness, brokenness, unforgiveness, bitterness, and mistrust that threaten to tear you apart. These deadly emotions will kill the root of your marriage. These poisonous seeds are very destructive if allowed to grow. They must be plucked up in the early stages when they are tender and young. How do you get rid of these enemies of your sacred union? Through prayer, fasting, love, forgiveness and understanding between two hearts that seek to heal and conquer but never divide.

GROWTH IS INEVITABLE

Because we were married at such a young age (I was eighteen; he was twenty), there were signs of abusive behaviors that I didn't become aware of until I was much older. I was too young and naive to really understand that in every relationship, there should be boundaries set.

Individuals will grow. It's deadly to become intimidated by the growth that must take place; growth is a necessity. In the eyes of my ex-husband, I was his sweet, little girl bride who was submissive, obedient, and hung on to every word he said.

There comes a time when the growth process takes place for the betterment of the individual. It also brings something new and beneficial to the relationship. I was a hard worker, and I reaped the fruits of my labor. I owned and operated a preschool yielding over six figures a year and was able to purchase our first home. This success came because of the schooling, training, and growth I acquired. I transitioned from being an employee to an employer. Anything that doesn't grow becomes stagnant, and I wanted to grow.

WHITE TULIPS

White tulips are a symbol of forgiveness, of being renewed and restored. Forgiveness gives one the ability to bounce back from heartache, pain, brokenness, and disappointment. It allows one to experience resilience through challenges because when you forgive, you live.

As a little girl growing up in Reno, Nevada, my mother and I would plant tulips. I remember one season it was very cold from the snow and ice. Even though the snow eventually melted, the ground where we planted the tulips was very, very hard. I thought to myself, *Our flowers won't be able to grow through this.* But one day, when we returned home from our daily activities, I discovered some things budding in the ground. To my surprise, the tulips persevered. That spoke volumes to me. It said that even though it seems impossible for anything good to grow out of the hardness in our lives, with resilience, we have the capacity to make it happen.

That tulip's ability to grow back season after season made me think about myself. Even though I endured some hard places, I bounced back. If I can do it, anyone can. You are beautiful, but if your ability to grow has a cap on it, you cannot fulfill the purpose within you. It will gradually diminish your self-esteem and cripple you.

Perhaps, you do not even understand the path you are journeying on right now. Nevertheless, you must put your trust in God and believe that He is definitely up to something great concerning your life. God loves you and will be with you every step of the way. Just keep the faith because a new reality of great things awaits you. It is so! In Jesus' name. Amen.

> ### DECLARATION
>
> In life, we will experience unexpected challenges. However, we must always trust and depend on God knowing He will bring us through the hard, embarrassing, and ugly circumstances.
>
> Make your declaration that as a woman of integrity, you will remain faithful, steadfast, and unmovable… He will take care of our business as we continue to draw closer to Him. We will survive. We will overcome, and we will live again.
>
>> Therefore, my beloved brethren, be ye stedfast, unmoveable, always abounding in the work of the Lord, forasmuch as ye know that your labour is not in vain in the Lord. (1 Corinthians 15:58)

> ### PRAYER
>
> Dear heavenly Father, I come to You in need of comfort. I know there are times when You can take our lives to give us Your life. I may not understand everything, but I know that You know everything. I believe You will lead and guide me through difficult, crushing circumstances. I will emerge anointed to be used by You and to make a difference in the lives of others. Give me the courage to grow and blossom into what you have called me to be. I yield my life to Your perfect will. In Jesus' name, I pray. Amen.

CHAPTER 2

THE PROCESS

In life, there are many lessons to be learned. We can choose to apply what we have learned or we can continue to repeat the same mistakes, living in frustration. At times, it's the process of being taught the lesson that we want to avoid, which in some cases brings pain before it yields healing. So we settle back into what's comfortable and familiar.

> And be not conformed to this world: but be ye transformed by the renewing of your mind, that ye may prove what is that good, and acceptable, and perfect, will of God. (Romans 12:2)

Being transformed by the renewing of your mind requires a conscious decision to surrender your will and desires to God's will and desires. However, the problem in doing so is that you will experience the war between the spirit and the flesh. This is an inward battle that will challenge you to grow and mature through trials that are uniquely designed for you. I like to think of it as God being the master life tailor who knows all of our measurements and limitations. He knows how much we can bear and how long or short our trials need to be.

Every circumstance is different, so you can be confident in the fact that when He completes a work in you, you are going to be equipped and perfectly designed to do the ministry He has tailor-made for you. The process is difficult to withstand, but I declare you must withstand. You can't give up!

> Finally, my brethren be strong in the Lord, and in the power of His might. Put on the whole armor of God, that ye may be able to stand against the wiles of the devil. (Ephesians 6:10–11)

DRESSED FOR SUCCESS

If you're not dressed, you can't stand against the wiles of the Devil. Wherever the Enemy is fighting you the most is the area you have left uncovered in your life. The Bible implores us to put on the whole armor of God that we may be able to stand. If the Enemy keeps attacking your mind, you need to *put on the helmet of salvation* to rebuke and cast out every idle thought of torment, unrest, fear, doubt, confusion, and lust, to overcome him. Replace those thoughts with what the Word instructs us to do.

> Finally, brethren, whatsoever things are true, whatsoever things are honest, whatsoever things are just, whatsoever things are pure, whatsoever things are lovely, whatsoever things are of good report; if there be any virtue, and if there be any praise, think on these things. (Philippians 4:8)

Put on the breastplate of righteousness to protect your heart and vital organs. Believe it or not, your health and well-being are connected to what is in your heart. Therefore, you should maintain a pure and righteous heart that seeks to be right and do right in the sight of God. Harboring toxic emotions like hatred, unforgiveness, bitterness, and such like destroys you. You can also reap the benefits of experiencing real joy, inner peace, true love, and faith if you eradicate those toxic emotions.

Gird up your loins with truth. To thine own self be true. It can be challenging when you find yourself alone and without companionship. You long to be loved and starve for affection. It can be a serious struggle. Nevertheless, fight on and do what is right. Cry out to God for help. Stay accountable to someone who will pray with you and keep you on task. Stay busy and involved with healthy activities that occupy your mind. You can stand if you truly want to.

Keep your feet shod with the preparation of the gospel of peace. Mind what you do and where you go. These challenging times will compose your testimony. They are the stories you will tell about how God brought you through and where He is taking you. You will experience great resistance from the Enemy because of the promises of God's victorious Word that will be active in your life.

> *I declare you must withstand. You can't give up!*

Wherever you are, let your presence reflect Christ. Do not be quick to enter places that will bring your spirit down and ruin your day. Instead, surround yourself with people who love you and add to your life spiritually and emotionally without subtracting from you.

Keep the shield of faith to quench every fiery dart of Satan that attacks you. The shield will keep every dart from penetrating you. You must remember that weapons will be formed against you, but they will not prosper. So *take the sword of the Spirit* to speak and declare every promise of God in the atmosphere. His Word is infallible and will never fail. You can stand on His Word!

YOU ARE AN ANSWER

You are somebody else's answer. You are the key to someone else's breakthrough. God wants to use you to be an example to many others.

I know you may be saying, "Lord it's not fair. Why do I have to suffer to help somebody else?" It's painful; it hurts, and it's very uncomfortable. However, kicking and screaming will only delay the process you must go through. Trust me, sooner or later, when you're done piloting your own life, you will discover that God has His way anyway. Will you submit, grow up, and enjoy the journey with new discoveries about your relationship with God? Or will you prolong the process while you fester, anger and lament about your unfulfilling, stagnant, complacent condition? The choice is yours, but take comfort in knowing that God will not put more on you than you can bear.

> Come unto me, all ye that labour and are heavy laden, and I will give you rest. Take my yoke upon you, and learn of me; for I am meek and lowly in heart: and ye shall find rest unto your souls. For my yolk is easy, and my burden is light. (Matthew 11:28–30)

LET IT GO

Whatever your burden is, give it to God. Whatever you're afraid of or holding on to, let it go. Ask yourself, *What changes do I need to make to really hear from God? Do those changes make me feel isolated, alone, different, lost, unattractive or out of place?*

You must understand that our different ministries may require different sacrifices. If you don't, it may hinder your progress. It may keep you from hearing from God or receiving the level of anointing you have been asking God for. It can even hinder you from getting the strategy and direction you want Him to give you for your life. Search your heart with honesty to receive the answer.

One thing I've learned is when God reveals the answers to you, but you fail to obey, it is an indication that whatever you are holding on to is more important than the assignment God has for you.

How much time do you think you have left on this earth? If you can't answer that question, then tell me, why are you wasting time? Why aren't you lining up with God's call and assignment for your life? Are you crippled by fear and doubt? Are you afraid to step out of your comfort zone into the unknown? Cast out those doubts and fears; walk out your purpose with confidence and authority. As you trust God and move forward, He will manifest His glory through your obedience.

Don't be fazed if the progress you imagined is not happening the way you desired. Don't look at your beginning stages as if they are insignificant. God is delighted when we do His will. Our beginning stages develop the greater things within us.

NEVER RETREAT

In the story of David and Goliath, we find that David was confident he could defeat Goliath because of the encounters he had while tending the sheep. When the time came to go up against Goliath, David testifies of how he slew a lion and a bear, and delivered a sheep out of the lion's mouth.

> I come to thee in the name of the Lord of hosts, the God of the armies of Israel, whom thou hast defied. This day will the Lord deliver thee into mine hand... all the earth may know that there is a God in Israel. And all this assembly shall know that the Lord saveth not with sword and spear: for the battle is the Lord's, and he will give you into our hands. (1 Samuel 17:45-47)

Like David, you must open your mouth and declare your victory. You have already operated in your assignment, so take courage. Remind yourself and the Enemy why you won't retreat. Enough is enough! Your life, family, church, and community are at stake and waiting for you to do what God has given you to do.

In David's eyes, conquering Goliath was a small thing because his faith in God was great. I declare that your faith will be great too. We can all look back over our lives and see where God has shown Himself strong.

I know if it had not been for the Lord, I could have lost my mind. I could have done something I would have regretted for the rest of my life. I was extremely hurt and angry because the man I spent almost twenty years of my life with was slandering my name and my character. He was treating me like a woman he never even knew or as if I had never borne one of his children. It left me broken, angry, and devastated. If I had retaliated as I wanted to, I would have aborted my purpose and ministry, along with hurting the family and friends I loved. But God!

When my ex launched his attack against me on social media by spreading lies to mar my reputation and demean me (the mother of his five children), I thought, *Lord, how could You let this be? Do You care?* He was an ex NFL football player as well as a pastor, so this gave him a platform to further abuse me publicly. It hurt me knowing that he had the voice through media to tear me apart, emotionally. I believe that it was the prayers of those who loved me, my family that helped me to be shielded when the fiery darts were thrown my way. It enabled me to be strong at a time when I just wanted to give up, but to God be the glory I was covered under the blood of Jesus. I survived. My ex went on TV interviews and radio shows, preaching here and there, influencing people to believe that I (his ex-wife) had been unfaithful to him. I wondered if those people entertaining his campaign (who claimed to have a relationship with God) possessed *any* discernment.

It reminded me of high school days. You would hear about the young boys degrading the girls they slept with. They would tell all their friends what happened to make themselves look good and the young girl look bad.

The only difference is I was married to this man, which made his behavior far more humiliating and gut-wrenching. I promised myself as a young girl that I would save myself for my husband, which I did. So I was devastated this happened to me. Talk about ironic! The very thing I feared as a young girl happened to me as an adult. The one closest to me hurt me very badly, but I survived.

I AM A SURVIVOR

As I began entreating God, He gave me the strength not to retaliate against the wrong I felt was done to me. I had to shut down every negative and degrading conversation that was being spoken or posted on social media to regain my victory and my peace. I was soon reminded that at the beginning of the divorce proceedings, God told me He would fight for me. I can't tell you how many times I had to declare to the Enemy what God said. At this point, I was challenged to stand still and trust God.

I can't begin to tell you of all the emotional and mental trauma, as well as abusive experiences I was put through. I recall the nights when I cried uncontrollably. I felt as if a weight sat on my chest sucking the air out of my lungs and suffocating me. I wanted to flee to a place where nobody could ever find me. Yet, something within willed me to keep fighting. Whenever I was at my wit's end, God would encourage me through His Word. I would find myself with my hands raised crying out to God. That gave me the breakthrough and the extra strength I needed to make it through.

Another amazing experience I encountered was getting the assurance that everything was okay when I worshiped God. It took the sting out of every negative emotion and gave me a sense of peace and comfort. Immediately, my problems and issues didn't seem as great as I thought they were.

My children were split up and got caught in the crossfire of chaos. They were being told that I didn't love them anymore. That broke my heart, confused, and shocked me.

We have all been through some rough places. I encourage you to look at yourself in the mirror and declare these words with power and authority: *I am a survivor!*

What the Enemy devised to destroy me and take me out, God blocked it! I am a survivor destined to thrive, prosper, flourish, and grow vigorously with full vital strength.

THE LETTER

I was staying with my mother for a while trying to get through the trauma and remain strong for my younger daughters who were living there with me at that time. On June 7, 2014, I was going through a folder looking for my daughter's birth certificate. To my surprise, I came across a twenty-page letter that was written to me by my ex. It caught my attention because I recognized his handwriting.

Our divorce was finalized on March 31, 2011, and the letter was dated August 8, 2011, with the time it was written on it. I found the letter exactly one day before what would have been our twenty-third wedding anniversary.

As I read the letter, I cried uncontrollably, so much so that my daughter kept asking me, *Mom, are you okay?* I couldn't even speak. But that was the day of my deliverance. God broke some very heavy demonic chains that kept me in bondage because of the lies that were being spoken about me.

What caught my attention was that my ex had already bound his tongue, which spoke every evil word against me. He declared, and I quote, "That every word should be stricken forever in the skies around us and the skies of our mind and never be released to speak those killer words again." He also apologized and told me he knew he had hurt me with his jealous ways. He said he was sorry for falsely accusing me. In this letter, he wrote the truth from his heart and took responsibility for his wrongdoing.

He had stopped saying anything good about me as a woman. I mean, the compliments stopped; instead, I was being torn down in ways that were unthinkable. However, inside the letter, he told me what a beautiful woman, mother, and wife I was. I didn't matter whether or not I ever heard an apology from his lips. God allowed me to find this letter and thus began major healing for me.

> No weapon that is formed against thee shall prosper, and every tongue that shall rise against thee in judgment thou shalt condemn. This is the heritage of the servants of the Lord, and their righteousness is of me, saith the Lord. (Isaiah 54:17)

ACTIVATE YOUR FAITH

Being human means we will experience various emotions in our difficult seasons. That's okay. But do you really want to get God's attention then activate your faith? Faith moves God. It shows Him we trust Him enough to take our hands off the situation, so He can handle it and receive the glory. Regardless of who may have wronged or hurt us, we must remain focused. We must realize the problems are distractions to offset our purpose. The more I began to pray for my ex-husband, the more I realized he was hurting just like me, but he was dealing with it in the wrong way.

I know you have heard the expression, "Hurting people hurt people." I began to have compassion for his soul because he wasn't the same man I once knew. On the flip side, his actions ignited a fire within me. It spurred me on to do the ministry that was always dwelling inside, which I was afraid to pursue. I experienced a major growth spurt.

His actions didn't kill me. In fact, I am stronger than I ever was, a work in progress, striving to do bigger and better things.

God will never leave us alone. Many days, we will feel lonely, down-spirited, and weak, but God is holding us. I love the passage of Scripture where Jesus was speaking to Simon Peter:

> Simon, Simon, behold, Satan hath desired to have you, that he may sift you as wheat: But I have prayed for thee, that thy faith fail not: and when thou art converted, strengthen thy brethren. (Luke 22:31–32)

How awesome it is that Jesus is praying for us. Like Simon Peter, we want to please God with all our hearts, but sometimes we fail Him and miss the mark. However, whatever you do, keep the faith. Go through your test. When you have repented and turned to God for help, strengthen your brothers and sisters; encourage them to keep the faith.

DECLARATION

I declare that I will trust the Lord with all my heart and lean not on my own understanding. I realize the process is necessary so I can grow as a result of the hard challenges that come to make me stronger. So I declare that I will stand on the Word of God believing that all things are working together for my good, no matter what it looks like or how I feel. The victory is already mine. I declare it to be so. In Jesus' name. Amen.

PRAYER

Lord Jesus, I come before You with an open heart and an ear to hear directly from You. It is my desire to please You in everything that I do. Give me the grace to be patient and embrace the process that is uniquely designed for me to reach the next level of my destiny. I trust You, Lord, and submit to Your perfect will. In Jesus' name, which is above all other names, I pray. Amen.

CHAPTER 3

FRUIT OF THE SPIRIT

Stop picking my fruit! Stop picking my fruit! I loved him, and I thought he loved me too. I was a happy-go-lucky, giddy, and carefree young lady full of destiny, promise, and charisma. My spirit was being crushed, and I couldn't understand why. Being young and in love without understanding the game of life or having any real-life experiences can paint you a picture of false reality. You are as naive as the day is long.

The red flags waving in the wind looked like party decor to me; it was my norm. I didn't know I needed to fix what was wrong because it felt so right! Whatever he said was the final word. It wasn't really a marital partnership; it was his world. I was his little girl bride, until one day I grew up, and he noticed! It changed our lives forever.

I became fearful of the man I once loved with all my heart. His jealous and insecure ways made him unbearable to live with. He was now on a mission to prevent any growth from taking place in my life. I felt inadequate, lonely, and hurt. The subtle verbal, mental, emotional, and psychological abuse was in full force. This didn't happen overnight; it was a process. I tried to fight for myself with all my might! I cried. I prayed. I tried to convince him that I loved him but to no avail.

The nights were long and sleepless. With a racing heart, afraid of what could happen, I silently prayed asking God to cover and protect me. *How could this happen to me? To us?* We were supposed to be a team or so I thought.

Not only was he the father of our children, he was my pastor too! I knew I could never tell anybody what I was really going through. This man knew the Word of God and was very influential. He had a gift to impart into God's people, so my voice remained silent. These overwhelming feelings left me hopeless, defeated, and as tired as a marathon runner with no finish line in sight. All the while, my fruit was being diminished. I desperately needed *Jehovah Rapha*, the Lord Who heals.

MY DECLARATION

I declare that I am loving, faithful, and loyal. I am a great wife. I am a wonderful mother, sister, and friend. I am living with great expectations from God! I am who God says I am even when others around me try to define who I am in a negative light. What God says and thinks about me matters more than what anybody else could ever say or think.

> For I know the thoughts that I think toward you, saith the Lord, thoughts of peace, and not of evil, to give you an expected end. (Jeremiah 29:11)

After my marriage failed, I had to develop the fruit of the Spirit. I love God, and as I went through the process of divorce, I found out I needed more development. I thought I had all the love, joy, peace, long-suffering, and other marvelous fruit I needed. But I was wrong.

I discovered that the devastation, hurt, and pain I felt were causing the fruit I thought I had enough of to dry up and fall away.

Reaching this point, I had to ask God to give me more love and not to let my circumstances dictate how my heart felt. This was tough because I was married to my children's father for almost twenty years. We married young and started a ministry together about seven years or so into our marriage. We pastored together for eleven years and had five children. I never imagined that my journey would cause me to evolve into the person I started to become. But thank God for Jesus and the blood of the Lamb.

It was a nightly routine for him to badger me because of the jealous thoughts that filled his head. He would even shake me violently out of sleep to answer questions that haunted his imagination. He interrogated me about things he perceived to be true but that were lies. They weren't based on reality but on what his tormented mind conjured up.

> *The red flags waving in the wind looked like party decor to me.*

Anxiety, fear, and depression became my companions, but somehow, I had enough fight left, and I decided to work on me. I worked out every day. I even sought counseling to release all the pain that I was bottling up inside. I was severely wounded because the man I thought I knew was no longer the same. That caused me to feel less joy, peace, love, kindness, and goodness.

My soul was being crushed. However, in the midst of the chaos, I noticed a change in me. I fell out of love with the man I had loved for so many years. I felt very disconnected from him in a way I had never experienced. It felt cold and lonely, but I began a journey of my own. I severed a lot of ties in my heart. That was a major transition for the relationship.

I was constantly tormented whenever we were out in public. If other couples left before us when we were on dinner dates, he would say I made them uncomfortable, and they could no longer stay. It was all my doing he would say. I felt like a punished, scolded child who would have to deal with his wrath when we got home.

BE A TREE THAT BEARS FRUIT

As a child of God, I had to understand that when I was faced with challenging circumstances that attempted to diminish my peace and destroy my character, the fruit from my tree was being picked. Every cruel look and verbally abusive word plucked my joy, yanked my peace, and snatched my love. The eye-squinting glance reinforced there was no goodness in me. My fruit were ripped off without a care. I was left with the rigid ends of weakened branches. I was that tree.

What I had to give was forcefully being taken away. I could not produce from the very soul that had caused me to thrive, live, and pursue the goals, visions, and purpose for my life. I had to determine how the story was going to change. If I had nothing to give or live for, no purpose or vision, I would cease to exist naturally and spiritually. I needed spiritual CPR (cardiopulmonary resuscitation). I needed God to breathe life into me and cause the dead things within me to live again. I'm reminded of this parable:

> "A certain man had a fig tree planted in his vineyard, and he came seeking fruit on it and found none. Then he said to the keeper of his vineyard, 'Look, for three years I have come seeking fruit on this fig tree and find none. Cut it down; why does it use up the ground?' But he answered and said to him, 'Sir, let it alone this year also, until I dig around it and fertilize it. And if it bears fruit, well. But if not, after that you can cut it down.'" (Luke 13:6-9 NKJV)

In the natural sense, a tree that bears fruit can sustain life, give shade, and profit others. It can feed hungry people. In the spiritual sense, the fruit that you bear can assist you in maintaining your grace and dignity as a believer in Christ because you have the Spirit of God that governs you.

In the parable above, the gardener agreed to work with the tree one more year and if it bears fruit, fine, but if not, that's fine also. His solution to the problem of barrenness was to pay extra attention to the tree. He would fertilize and dig around it to see how it would respond.

THE DIGGING PROCESS

Digging around the tree is done to prevent root diseases that can kill the tree. Like the gardener, you need to preserve the life in you by doing some digging. The digging opens up the soil so the water can penetrate. You will replenish yourself as the water of the Word of God flows through your life. Enduring this process takes the faith to believe you still have something to live for. You must believe that you shall live and not die and go on to declare the works of the Lord according to Psalm 118:17. Allow the healing to take place.

Your life is not over! Fight through this process with a vengeance. Battle until you feel your energy and your drive come back. Resurrect the goals and dreams you had from the beginning.

The Enemy wants to destroy the seed God planted in you. Isn't it interesting that the Enemy will make you think that the very thing that gives you life is too overwhelming to tackle? No matter what negative thoughts float through your head, but you must put on strength.

The digging-around process will also cause you to examine yourself and discover what you're really made of. Are you going to lie down and let your disappointments kill you? Or are you going to get a healthy mind, body, and soul? You may look well put together on the outside, but you know there is deep-rooted damage that others cannot see. Only God can heal you.

THE RELOCATING PROCESS

During this process, the people who love you will help you move to a suitable place or environment through prayer and fasting. They do so to ensure that you are cared for and nurtured until you can adapt to your new location. For some, that location can mean a healthy place emotionally, mentally, and psychologically or just a safe haven from a physically abusive relationship.

In the natural sense, the key component of successfully relocating a tree is to move it with the root ball attached. For you, the root ball is your testimony of redemption. To get your bearings back, you must be planted in God and His Word daily. This allows His Word to take root in your heart to remind you of where He has brought you from and where He is taking you. Your eyes will begin to open, and you will understand who you are as a child of God. You are fearfully and wonderfully made. You are a beautiful person inside and out, full of self-worth, purpose, and destiny.

Naturally, a tree must be planted and nurtured for one year. Then, it can take root, mature, and grow while sustaining itself through the natural elements (sun, rain, dew, and snow). Those who commit to helping you – your close spiritual family and friends who are interceding for you and to whom you are accountable – must nurture you for one year. They must do so through the Word of God until you know you have the power of God working inside you to stand against the wiles of the Devil. This must continue until you begin to activate your faith and stand on the Word of God without doubt and fear, believing that God is in control of your destiny.

THE FERTILIZING PROCESS

The key people in this process are your spiritual caretakers. After you've experienced a traumatic situation, those who pour into you spiritually play a major role in your recovery.

> It shall be health to thy navel, and marrow to thy bones. (Proverbs 3:8)

The Word of God will bring healing to you. Are you receiving counseling to aid in your nurturing process? Remember, during this process, you must respond with obedience and trust in God to obtain the desired results. Submit your ways unto the Lord as opposed doing things your own way. Each phase is an opportunity for you to develop the fruit of the Spirit.

> Let this mind be in you, which was also in Christ Jesus. (Philippians 2:5)

You will begin to take on the mind of Christ and regain consciousness of your being both spiritually and naturally. You will understand your former state of mind and dislike what you became to survive. The Word of God will show you how much love the Father has for you. It will reveal just how much we are living beneath our privileges when we allow others to abuse, disrespect, dishonor, degrade, and mistreat us.

> What? Know ye not that your body is the temple of the Holy Ghost which is in you, which ye have of God, and ye are not your own? For ye are bought with a price: therefore glorify God in your body, and in your spirit, which are God's. (1 Corinthians 6:19-20)

We are the King's kids; therefore, we should live by kingdom principles and enjoy kingdom living. You have a right to enjoy your life today.

It is important for us to glorify God with our conduct, what we allow to enter our eye gates, ear gates, and our mouths. We must also be wary of abusing or allowing others to abuse our temples; we belong to God.

THE PRUNING PROCESS

Pruning is essential to the health of the tree because it removes dead, damaged, and diseased branches. This helps prevent insects and decaying organisms from entering the tree. As a result, it allows the tree to grow and increase in fruitfulness.

You need to do some pruning in your life. It is time to cut off toxic relationships with people who do not have your best interest at heart. These people are defeatist and feed you with negative energy to keep you emotionally damaged. They never seem to have anything positive or uplifting to pour into you because they are spiritually dead, damaged, and diseased; misery loves company. Their negative conversations do not evoke healing or productivity; they neither edify God nor you.

The pruning process may be painful and uncomfortable, but it will enhance what is already in you. It will help you to mature and reach a more productive and abundant place in your life.

As you are pruned, you will experience a test that will give you a testimony. You will recognize areas in your life that have become more refined and be prepared to help others to grow.

You must remove all the suckers from your life. In the natural, suckers thrive on the parts of the tree that are wounded; they deplete the tree of nutrients. So when you experience a sudden loss of joy, peace, love, something or someone toxic is depleting you of what God wants to accomplish in your life.

Suckers will feed you with information to hurt you even though they are well aware that you are going through a healing process. Most times, it is done to see how bad they can make you feel. Guard your heart; guard your spirit, and elevate your mind with good things. Don't let the suckers suck the life out of you.

> **PRAYER**
>
> Lord, thank You for the wisdom, knowledge, and understanding to know the difference between abuse and love. Thank You for awakening my innermost being to love myself the way You have shown love toward me. Thank You for caring for me and covering me in every situation. I thank You for peace and real joy because it is your strength that helps to sustain me when I am feeling weak and unable to push forward. Thank You for the digging process that destroys the disease of sin. Thank You for the relocating process that has helped to move me to a suitable place through prayer and fasting. Thank You for fertilizing my soul through Your infallible Word. Thank You for pruning me, so that I can be in a more abundant place in my life to receive from You. In Jesus' name, I pray. Amen.

CHAPTER 4

BARBIE DOLL

Barbie has everything! The man, the children, the house, the career, the car, and the clothes. All the extra amenities to make life fun, sweet, and comfortable are hers. *Or are they?* One thing about Barbie is that she can represent any woman at any stage in her life whether good, bad or ugly.

Some people assess their friends and family based on the things they desire, not having the complete picture of the things they see. For example, if a woman who desires stability and security sees another woman with a man who has a job, but her man doesn't, she will envy that one thing she lacks. She has no idea if the man she admires is a responsible person who handles his money or business affairs wisely. All she knows is that he has a job.

Very often, we admire people based on a perceived lack in our lives and relationships. So you look at how well kept someone's wife is and wish you were her. She has nice clothes; she's talented, and she always looks happy every time you see her. However, you don't know what she has to do to keep her sanity. Her home life may be in turmoil, but she can't let anyone else know it. She tries hard not to break under the pressure. Her efforts to hold things down for everybody else, cover for her man, hope, pray, and wait for things to change overwhelm her.

Does this sound like someone you know? Is that person trying to cover up what some people can already see? Well, I call this the Barbie Doll Syndrome, and I had it. I was trying to be who and what everybody needed me to be, but things couldn't have been more dysfunctional. Underneath it all, I didn't have a clue.

As I said before, I married my children's father at the age of eighteen. It was my first real relationship. He was the first man I ever knew on an intimate level, and he was my world.

I moved straight out of my parents' home into his home. I left California and moved to Phoenix, Arizona where we began our lives together. All I knew was to do all I could to support him, let him be the man who runs our household and the one who makes the final decisions.

Was this all bad or wrong? No! But when someone's submission is taken advantage of, it can become a real nightmare. I thought I was being the submissive wife the Bible talks about. Boy, was I wrong.

Now that I look back, we really weren't a team at all. It was his way or no way, but that didn't really matter to me. I loved him. I was young, and it was the way I was being raised by him. After all, I was his Barbie doll.

CHANGE IS CONSTANT

As the years went on, life and time were bringing about changes in my life. Yes, change! The one thing he could not control was the fact that in life, things change, and it doesn't have to be for the worst. In my case, I was evolving into my womanhood. I enjoyed dressing and doing girly things like my hair and my nails because now, I could financially afford to do something nice for me. My kids were getting older, and I was contributing to our household.

Who you are as a young adult is not who you will be as you grow and mature. Anything that does not grow is stagnant because it does not progress. When you are held back from making healthy changes in your life, it can affect you as a person. It can cause you to lose your self-esteem, your vibrant personality, the light in your eyes, your joy and peace. You become untrue to who you really are.

The main characteristic of a Barbie is that she is lifeless but looks full of life. She has eyes, but she cannot see. She has ears, but she cannot hear. She has lips, but she cannot speak. You dress her and fix her any way you would like. What happens when all of a sudden, she begins to breathe? What do you do when she shows unexpected signs of life and she discovers who she is and what she is made of? She begins to fight for her life by asking some very tough questions.

> *I was trying to be who and what everybody needed me to be.*

In many situations, we must take some responsibility for allowing ourselves to become stranded in unhealthy relationships. What is your excuse? I never asked my husband to be accountable even when he was wrong because I wanted peace. I wanted to move forward, thinking that was the godly thing to do.

Now, don't get it twisted; you should always use wisdom when dealing with your mate. I would apologize for things that I didn't do wrong. This didn't show how awesome I was as a wife. Instead, it showed how insecure I was. I didn't understand this until later in life.

THE NEW NORMAL

I regret that I allowed uncorrected behavior to continue just to get him to be his "normal" self. I would give in to get him off the couch and back in the bedroom to sleep with me. I wanted to continue having conversations even when he didn't want to talk. He held back his words of affection and comfort as a way of punishing me, as well as letting me know he was in control and angry. When *he* was ready, we would communicate.

Among other reasons, we had children together. I wanted to protect them and keep things "normal" for them. I came from a home where my parents loved each other and stayed together until my father passed away. I never looked at divorce as an option even though I was in a very abusive relationship. At that time, I didn't consider it to be abusive. I just figured that he was who he was and made excuses for him. After all, he was the disciplinarian, and I was always the one in trouble.

Lastly, if I left him, we had a whole church family who was going to know that we weren't as perfect as we looked. So I continued to cover up for him because I expected God to work it out. But remember, it takes two to make a thing go right. The fault was not in God; it was in us. I must admit, at this stage, I was so tired of being hurt that I had no more fight left in me. No matter how exhausted I was, he wanted to try to go another round. This was part of his vicious cycle where he would always apologize for things he said and did. He would promise me that he would never do anything to hurt me again and even make me cry. He would give me gifts and show love and affection to make me feel like things were safe and secure again. Once I finally figured it out, the emotional roller coaster ride left me hurt and confused.

A Barbie's life is not what it's all cracked up to be. The crazy thing here is I wasn't the one who filed for a divorce. To be honest with you, he had no biblical grounds to file for divorce. Yet, I believe that all things are still working together for my good, no matter how bad it hurts sometimes. I know that God is still in control, and He will bring me to my expected end, so I anticipate great things.

THE PURSUIT OF PURPOSE

If you have ever experienced the Barbie Doll Syndrome that has caused you to shut down on life, purpose, destiny, and your goals, I encourage you to persevere. Don't let anything stop you from doing what God has called you to do. When you do not operate in your gifts, you become unfulfilled. Do you wonder why certain things are not working out in your favor as they should. It's because you are not operating in your purpose.

Each one of us has a purpose. In our pursuit of that purpose, we touch and change the lives of other people. This is what the Enemy is afraid of. He does not want people who will be changed through your life to ever come in contact with you. Once their lives are changed, they will become inspired, and they too will go out and connect with other people who will become passionate about their purpose and win more souls for Christ.

Decide to be more than a pretty face and a fashion guru. Become a woman of substance, character, and integrity. Begin speaking the truth, walking after God's heart and living by His Word. Some women are doing all they can not to lose themselves. If that's you, allow me to encourage you: You can make it sister!

I pray God ignites your passion for your family. May He give you wisdom as you raise your children and love your man of God to the point at which he can't help but reciprocate agape love to you.

THE ROOT

I later came to understand that the trauma of his parents' divorce was never dealt with and stopped time for him. This caused him to be impaired in his ability to cultivate our marriage and our relationship through our challenges. He didn't have the tools needed to hold things together. It was during the early to mid-years of marriage that unhealthy behaviors (that were always there) began to manifest in major ways.

He dictated what I wore, where I went, and who I could and could not go with. His abuse caused me to believe that everything that went wrong in our relationship was my fault. Nonetheless, through prayer, counseling, and support from my family and friends, I came to understand that I could only be accountable for myself. I could not hold myself responsible for his actions. I released myself from that burden, and the only thing that I had to make sure of was that I lived with no regrets.

I would pray to God to help me forgive him every chance I got, no matter how hurtful or devastating his words would be. It was hard to believe that such cruel words could come from the lips of the man who would also use his words to comfort me, heal me, speak life into me, and honor me.

At eighteen years old, I was growing up and becoming a beautiful young woman whom he did not want to lose. As we grew older, the thought and fear of him losing me grew – so did the hell that was breaking loose in our home. Instead of trying to bring things together that would help us to heal, it seemed his focus was more on getting me to change as a remedy for our problems. He was handsome and all that I desired, but he didn't know how to embrace us changing together.

Upon reflection, I hurt for the young man inside of him. He was never able to resolve the issues within himself to be the husband and father my children and I needed when a crisis hit our home. All he knew was how to keep things together according to *his* way – being in control.

WAIT... WHAT?

It became more apparent to me that something was wrong when he threw me a surprise thirtieth birthday celebration with a bounce house and a Barbie cake. I guess it was appropriate at that time because, after all, I was his Barbie doll.

In retrospect, my growth was stunted just like his. I never really challenged anything that he said or did. In fact, even if I tried, he would quickly shut me down with his powerful authoritative words. As far as both of us were concerned, he was always right, and that's just how we flowed. He was our final answer. I admired, respected, and believed his every word.

I've learned that as a Barbie, you go with the flow, and when it is time to interact, Barbie is wherever you leave her, ready to be your ride or die.

The growing pains were wearing me out, so I sought counseling for both of us. However, both parties must want the same thing to get the results. Half of a heart is still a broken heart that can no longer be whole. Thankfully, the girl inside me began to outgrow the Barbie Doll Syndrome.

DECLARATION

I declare that I will focus on being the woman God is creating me to be, full of life with eyes to see the purpose and destiny for my life. My ears will hear and receive His Word in my heart, and my voice will speak declaring His promises over every situation in my life; it is so.

PRAYER

Dear Lord Jesus, we thank You for the beautiful women who may be experiencing the Barbie Doll Syndrome. You know every situation that they encounter. I speak life in their hearts, souls, and beings. Open their eyes and ears. Let praises be on their lips. Most importantly, let their hearts be open to receive You. Let them bring change to the kingdom of God through the power and anointing of Jesus Christ. From this day forward, we will walk in the authority You have given us to bring our purpose and our destinies to pass. We declare and decree it in the matchless name of Jesus. We are free! We are free! We are free! Amen.

CHAPTER 5

UNMUTE YOUR HEART

There is nothing worse than driving down the street on a beautiful day, feeling good, listening to your favorite song by your favorite artist, singing at the top of your lungs like you're in concert because you know all the riffs and runs, the instrumental cues and breaks in the song and feeling the rhythm throughout your entire body, when all of a sudden, the music stops. The silence catches you off guard and you sing off key. You didn't expect it and it kills the flow.

Flow is powerful. It is an ongoing forward motion, a steady stream of something. In nature, river flow plays a significant role in maintaining the proper balance of salt and mineral levels so that the aquatic life will not be affected. It prevents pollution and toxicity in the water. What would happen if the rivers stop flowing? Who would it affect? Everything and everyone who consumes or comes in contact with the toxic waste caused by stagnation.

So the bigger question is how long can you hold the toxic feelings of anger, unforgiveness, hatred, hurt, pain, or bitterness inside without polluting your soul? I'm going to park this right here and let you answer. It's okay. You can keep it 100 percent real with me.

If you have honestly come to terms with yourself and let toxic emotions flow out of you, then I thank God for His restoration power that's working in your life. However, if you know you need healing and freedom, today is your day. Be free and unmute your heart!

Yes, our hearts can be so cluttered with what happened to us and who did us wrong that those toxic emotions we justify can ultimately destroy us in the long run. They can cause people to avoid us because the festered hurt makes us unapproachable and unpleasant to be around. Sadly, we drown ourselves in the stale, putrid rivers of self-pity and loneliness.

I know you're hurting, but if you just keep moving and activate the Word of God in your life, you will receive the manifestation of your healing. There is no doubt that something or someone muted your heart, but you have the power and the right to unmute it. Turn up the volume on your voice that was silenced. Take back your life and live again. Praise God in advance for the victory because your mess needs to become your message of hope and restoration.

Take time to journal how you feel when you're at your lowest place. This may sound strange, but your lowest point may be the best place to be because when you're down, you can't go anywhere else but up. You can rebuild what was torn down.

THE TRIGGER EFFECT

What is triggering those overwhelming feelings of sadness? I found out that certain songs, events, people, and even situations would cause me to relapse into old, familiar, hurtful feelings that would change my mood and bring me down. This awareness allowed me to better prepare and fortify my mind with Scriptures, songs, and new strategies to overcome the challenges. You see, when you do the unexpected and prayerfully respond with new tactics that lift you above your

Chapter 5 ■ Unmute Your Heart

circumstances, the Enemy gets mad and confused because he can't destroy you.

I remember the day I decided to unmute my heart. I started off by journaling because the Lord instructed me to do so after my divorce was finalized in March 2011. I didn't understand why He even compelled me journal. First of all, I was not a big fan of writing. In high school, it took everything in me to even write an essay.

However, I was obedient to God, and I'm so glad today because of what the Lord has done through me. Now, the very trial I write about has given me so much compassion for families dealing with abuse. In these families, there is a need for renewal, healing, and restoration.

I know what it is like to vent to people and feel like you are a complete basket case. To make matters worse, some people don't really care. Let's face it. Some people want the juice, so they squeeze you like an orange to get the scoop. Then they run and tell everything.

How long can you hold the toxic feelings inside without polluting your soul?

Your true flow of release is forgiving and letting go. You must learn the valuable lessons your journey is meant to teach you. People don't want to be burdened with your self-pity because chances are, they are going through something themselves.

The funny thing about people is that we will all need help in one way or another. When you are in need of help yourself, you want to hear positive, uplifting words that can aid in your healing process. So people with negative energy are not welcomed.

While you are on the road to recovery through your unmuting process, you must shut out all negative conversations and people who are poisonous and toxic to you. You must build yourself up in your most holy faith, guarding and protecting your investment of time spent in the presence of God through prayer, fasting, and meditating on His Word. Shut out the darkness! Healing for your heart and entire body is found in the presence of the Lord. The minute you respond to the negative forces of anger, you deplete the joy, peace, and healing you have built up within you. So be mindful of your goal to heal and recover.

> The thief cometh not, but for to steal, and to kill, and to destroy: I am come that they might have life, and that they might have it more abundantly. (John 10:10)

> What shall we then say to these things? If God be for us, who can be against us? (Romans 8:31)

MAINTAINING OBEDIENCE

I learned that my unmuting process takes time and it doesn't happen overnight. You have to remain consistent in maintaining your obedience to God. If He has told you to stay away from certain people, places or things, be obedient. Rid yourself of toxic people or relationships; otherwise, you will relapse into doing the very things that will open your wounds and delay the healing process.

I remember as a little girl, I loved to ride my bike. On one occasion, I fell off and bruised my knee really bad. For a while, it was tender and sore to touch. During the healing process, the stiffness of the knee restricted my ability to walk properly, and the wound would itch. I would give in to the urge to scratch instead of leaving the wound to heal. In the same way, the Enemy often tries to prevent or delay our healing. He creates a great urge in our hearts to focus on the things we should leave alone. However, if we are careful to stay focused on being healed and not on the temporary discomfort, we will be alright.

What am I saying? Be careful! Guard your heart with the Word of God and remain obedient throughout the unmuting process. Let God purge your heart and mind of unforgiveness, hurt, anger, and bitterness. Let Him give you a fresh start to build a healthy new you. To do so, you must keep praying, growing in His Word, evolving, and learning your strengths through your trials. God will not put more on you than you can bear.

> There hath no temptation taken you but such as is common to man: but God is faithful, who will not suffer you to be tempted above that ye are able; but will with the temptation also make a way to escape, that ye may be able to bear it. (1 Corinthians 10:13)

Therefore, even when life gets tough, keep moving forward because your victory is ahead of you.

DECLARATION

I declare freedom from every toxic emotion that will pollute my heart, mind, character, and the essence of who I am. I will unmute my heart to be in a position to receive God's purpose and plan for my life. This can only be done when I open my heart to receive His love, healing, forgiveness, and restoration. I declare this day that I am free.

PRAYER

Dear Father God, I present my heart to You: broken, muted, damaged, hardened, and bitter. Dear God, take my heart of stone and give me a heart of flesh. Breathe upon me now. Mend the brokenness and make me whole. Unmute my heart, and let Your love flow through it. Repair the damage that was inflicted by others, and let forgiveness be my medicine. Soften the hardened areas, and let life begin again. Give me the strength to release those secret desires that seem harmless but are blocking new encounters and preventing me from moving forward. Make the bitterness of my journey sweet through Your precious blood. In the matchless name of Jesus, I pray. Amen.

CHAPTER 6

CAN YOU HEAR ME NOW?

How many times have we heard, *Can you hear me now? Can you hear me now?* We are definitely in a mobile phone era. Not only do adults have mobile phones, but our young children do too. Whenever we ask the question *Can you hear me now?* it implies that there is a blockage in the communication. Perhaps there is too much background noise, a technical problem, the person may very well be trying to avoid you or is focused on something else.

Many times, while making decisions, we do not pay attention to wise counsel. If we do, we will avoid the eventful detours on our journey? I use the term *eventful* instead of *unnecessary* because God is in control of our destinies; therefore, there is a purpose for everything we go through. But if you are one of those people who reject godly counsel, how is it working for you? Leaving God out of the equation and operating in our own wisdom will cause a train wreck every time; trust me.

When we do not take heed to wise counsel or advice we are sure to make mistakes that will teach us valuable lessons that we must learn. Prayerfully, we will learn our lesson to keep from repeating the same vicious cycles and gain the tools needed to grow and build a better us.

Another important tool that we have is our intuition, that gut feeling that tells us when something is not quite right. When you find yourself at the crossroads of uncertainty, not knowing what to do, take my mother's advice: Continue to pray and seek God for an answer; do nothing until you know you've heard from Him.

Listen to me when I tell you not to rush the process. Do not be in a hurry to make things happen. In God's time, He will bring it all together. You will be glad you waited for Him. Your patience may prevent a broken heart, emotional and mental mind games, disappointments, frustration, stress, health issues, and several other painful outcomes.

Operate in God's divine will, not His permissive will. His divine will is His design for your life with added blessings. However, His permissive will is when we operate in our desires and God permits it. You are doing you, your way, no doubt learning more lessons that you need to learn until you get it together. I encourage you to observe the results of your actions. Use the lessons learned whether good, bad, or ugly to help someone else. We must learn at one point or another that our challenges are not just about us. They are also about those around us journeying in this life.

COMPOUNDING THE PROBLEM

One of the hardest challenges I have ever had to experience was when I did exactly what I am trying to warn you not to do. After my almost twenty-year marriage to my children's father was over and after many different efforts to salvage it, I made an impulsive decision to remarry. I just wanted things to be fixed, mended, and restored. I was in an emotional and unhealthy state of mind. I was married for half my life, and my mindset was to fix my problems by filling the void I had for my broken family to be whole again. But, I learned that was not the answer.

When you are experiencing emotional trauma that is not the time to make life-altering decisions. You will be misguided every time. When you realize what you've done, you can sink deeper into despair; you will feel lost and out of control. However, no matter how low the valley, you can climb your way to the top again with lots of prayer and hard work. You just have to keep fighting.

Looking back at that situation, it's clear to me that everyone who loves me and cares about me tried to tell me. They asked if I was sure and if I had prayed; they even told me to wait. I honestly felt like I knew what I was doing, and nothing they said stuck. I admit I had some reservations, but the desire to fix my situation was stronger than their words. I was curious to see if my answer was what I needed. I needed to explore. So I made my choice.

> *Leaving God out of the equation will cause a train wreck every time*

That marriage soon ended in divorce. I had complicated my life with a whole new situation on top of what I had been dealing with from the start. I never allowed myself to heal from the emotional, verbal, mental, and physical abuse that I had dealt with for years. Despite my efforts to try, I could not give any healthy nutrients to that relationship.

I went through counseling for depression and dealt with feelings of hurt, anger, hopelessness, helplessness, and disappointment. I now had to process two divorces and everything else in between, but thank God for my Savior Jesus. He rescued me from a horrible pit. Hallelujah! He gave me the victory. It didn't happen overnight. Oh no! I had to search for myself because I didn't know who I was, but I thank God for the foundation my parents gave me as a child. God became a closer friend to me.

My family is second to none. They are all very highly anointed and powerful men and women of God who prayed me through, cried for me, and wanted to take the pain away. But I had to go through it, and today, I am still making great strides.

Even if you feel like you are all alone, God is there. Let Him guide you through. Be patient, seek counseling and prayer from someone who loves God, has a sincere prayer life, and loves you too. This is not the time to sulk and feel sorry for yourself. Instead, it's the time to be aware of what you're going through and gain the tools needed to learn from your mistakes and move forward.

Pray for yourself then pray effectually and fervently for others. Encourage them to never give up because they too are victorious no matter what it looks like. If they don't hear you the first time, after they go through, ask them, *Can you hear me now?!*

I guarantee you, sooner or later, they will hear your voice loud and clear echoing in their ears. They will even become more sensitive to that internal compass from the Spirit of God that leads, guides, and gets us back on track. Once you have found your way then you can have compassion for others.

DECLARATION

I declare that I will now hear with understanding and the wisdom of God as I pray in His will. I will not let my emotions dictate my decisions or my heart misguide me. I declare I will be patient while waiting for answers from God. I will be anxious for nothing and rest in Him.

PRAYER

Heavenly Father, before I make any decisions regarding my future, I give You complete control of my life. I relinquish my will for Yours. You have already laid out my path, and You know the steps I must take. I love You with all my heart. My desire is to please and trust You even when I can't trace You or see Your hand at work in my life because Your ways are not mine. Have Your way today and every day of my life. In Jesus' name, I pray. Amen.

CHAPTER 7

THE STAR

What does your heart feel? What does your heart say?

Keep thy heart with all diligence for out of it are the issues of life. (Proverbs 4:23)

What are your deep-rooted issues? As I was writing this book, the Lord was dealing with me. He was instructing me how to convey my message to His people, so they can understand what I am saying, identify with it, and receive answers through God's Word and my experiences.

One day, I had to stop writing and ask myself, *What does my heart feel? Do I feel healed from the pain and hurt from my challenges?* My heart simply replied, *No, I do not feel totally healed. However, I will live and declare I am healed until I experience the total manifestation.* The beauty of it all was hearing the voice of the Lord say to me, *You are more than qualified to be a vessel that I can use to fulfill my purpose through you.*

Everybody's challenges are different but hurt is hurt no matter what caused it. No one can minimize the hurt you feel or tell you when it's time to stop hurting. Make it your daily assignment to surrender that hurt to the Lord. Cast your cares on Him, for He cares for you. I consulted God about my heart issue because I wanted to be authentic in relaying my message of hope to the people of God. I told God I wanted answers, and I wanted to hear from Him. He heard me.

July 29, 2015 started with prayer on a 5:00 A.M. conference call with my mother and my siblings like we have done every morning. But on that particular day, one of the last things my mother said at the close of the prayer was, *Lord, we are expecting a miracle today.* We were all in agreement, and we all went about our day.

My daughter Jada and I both had appointments scheduled with the doctor that morning. After our appointments, my daughter Jada who was nineteen at the time wanted to drive us to our next destination. She had a new license and was eager to drive. I agreed, and we were on our way. As we were leaving the doctor's office, in a vision, I saw God erase the words "hurt" and "pain." My eyes filled with tears, and I began to cry on the inside. Immediately, I became aware of what God was doing. He was continuing to heal me on the inside.

THE CAR AND THE STAR

My daughter and I were soon on the freeway. Being a new driver and all, while attempting to change lanes, she lost control of the car. We swerved from side to side, vigorously, and she was unable to gain control. It happened so fast, and all I could think at that time was, *Oh, my God!* We were helpless. It felt as if the brakes locked up. The car made a complete left-hand turn from the far right side of the freeway, and we skidded all the way into the carpool lane. We crashed into the center divider head-on totaling out my truck. I blacked out.

Eventually, I woke up to my daughter saying, *Mom, Mom.* She later told me that I was slumped over. I had no idea how long I was out, but I remember looking at her, seeing that she was okay and feeling

Chapter 7 ■ The Star

relieved. She said, *Mom, your head!* I put my head back down and opened my eyes to a pool of blood in my lap. It was dripping down my face; the front of my head was busted open. I felt faint and disoriented and was unable to move my left side because the pain was so severe. In spite of that, I softly said, *Thank You, Jesus* and pleaded the blood of Jesus over both of us.

At that time, I was unaware of my daughter's injuries, but it was a miracle that she only suffered from a cut under her right foot. God spared and protected our lives. I asked God as I sat there, *Lord, am I going to survive this?* Because I felt like I wanted to slip away.

I looked through the side door mirror, and I saw a car that looked just like my sister Leisa's car passing by. I wasn't sure if it was her or not, but it looked like her car. Immediately, I felt a peace come over me as if that was a sign that God was with me, and I was going to be all right. It turned out that it was my sister. I was still unable to move my left side and discovered later that I had broken my left shoulder and fractured it in two places. Miraculously, at no time did my head ever bother me. I couldn't even tell you what I hit my head on.

> *Make it your daily assignment to surrender that hurt to the Lord.*

The paramedics and the doctors asked me so many questions. All I could say was that it was not my head; it was my arm. Later on, I learned they had concerns that I could lose my memory because of where I hit my head and the impact, but God kept my mind.

Shortly after we arrived at the hospital, Leisa entered the room. I was so overwhelmed and relieved. I wanted to cry, and I could see she wanted to break down, but she didn't. I guess she held it together for my sake. I assumed it was the condition of my head that troubled her, and I thought, *Wow! I must really be messed up.*

For a day and a half, I didn't see my face, and my sister didn't want me to until I got my stitches. I agreed. When I did finally see my face, I wondered, *Is it going to look like this forever?* The scar was severely swollen and I had so many stitches. I wasn't upset. In my spirit, I could hear God telling me that it wasn't a scar; it was a star. I voiced it to my friend Michelle who was with me. She encouraged and agreed with me on what I had spoken.

During this time, God began to speak and deal with me. Leading up to the accident, most of the emotional trauma I dealt with stemmed from the malicious lies my ex told about me. It was designed to tear me down, mar my name and character, and ultimately destroy me. But God said no.

[These photos were taken after the car accident. Everytime I see them all I can say is, "Thank You, Jesus, for Your protection." I know that my daughter and I still have purpose. Fairfield, CA in July 2015.]

THE HORSE

When I went home later that evening, God showed me a vision of a horse. I dismissed it and threw it out of my mind for a while, thinking it was just me. However, He showed it to me a second time. Why did God give me this vision again? The Lord revealed the significance of the horse in relation to my life. He ministered to me and showed me that horses are powerful, graceful, beautiful, noble, strong, and free. As women of God, we should possess these characteristics.

- Power – We are women of power with the ability to influence and direct people
- Grace – We are women of grace who are elegant and walk in the favor of God
- Beauty – We are women of beauty with a combination of qualities that make us pleasant
- Nobility – We possess nobility and are quality women in character
- Strong – We are women of strength and courage
- Freedom – We walk in freedom, have the power to speak with authority and bring change to our circumstances. Anything we set our minds to do, we can accomplish.

Women of God, we are made of all these characteristics. When God spoke to me, He did not stop there. He also began to deal with me on a personal and deeper level.

Many horses have different markings on their faces in the middle of their foreheads where there is a white discoloration. They have various names for the discoloration, but the name I am referring to is called a star. Although it doesn't look like a star in shape at all, this permanent mark identifies to whom the horse belongs. No two horses in the world have a marking with the same shape. The coal specks and patterns within a diamond identify it as such. Similarly, the star on a horse's forehead identifies whose it is. The owner will always be able to know and claim what is rightfully his should the horse be stolen. God's revelation to me was that the scar on my forehead, which I now call "star," identified me as His own.

When people hurt those who belong to God, they are hurting God. He feels our sorrows and cares about what hurts us. To me, this meant I was free from the burden of hurt that was placed on me. You can be free too. Many people have similar needs in their lives. They need to be free from situations that bind them. We are caught up in the lies the Enemy tells us. Whose report will we believe?

BE SPECIFIC

There is no set strategy for having our needs met. As our individual needs are so are the methods of fulfilling them. I remember sitting in Sunday school one morning feeling very low in spirit. I can't recall what the lesson was even about. At that time, I was battling depression after my divorce. I remember sitting there inattentively when all of a sudden, the Lord began to deal with me about being healed, delivered, and free.

He reminded me who I was and Whose I was. He promised me that I could proclaim and declare every promise in His Word. He told me to be specific about what I desired from Him and to pray according to His will. God desires to set His people free with a strategic plan to loose us from the strongholds of Satan. Many people want to be free but don't know how. Some don't have enough faith to receive their freedom. Following are specific needs we can address in prayer:

Redemption – The ultimate freedom is His *redemption*. He redeemed us by gaining possession of His people in exchange for His life. He cleared the debt of sin through His powerful blood.

Deliverance – His *deliverance* power rescues us and sets us free from sin. It releases us from the power of Satan.

Liberation – Some people are in need of *liberation*. Liberation occurs when a person(s) has been set free from imprisonment, slavery, oppression, confinement, and bondage.

Discharged – Maybe you need to be *discharged*. You must be told that you can or must leave a place or situation.

Release – Let God enable you to escape the confinements of Satan and set you free from bondage. God did this for me, and I no longer have to carry the emotional burden I carried because He released me.

Rescue – Some of us need to be rescued from dangerous or distressing situations. I have found that when people have been in abusive situations, it is hard for them to make healthy decisions for themselves because of fear. Sometimes, they feel obligated to stay in unhealthy situations because of finances, children or even to maintain a reputation. If this is you, you need to be rescued. Those of us who have a relationship with Jesus Christ have the ability to rescue lives and help people who need to know there is a better way.

Emancipation – This is a process of being set free from legal, social or political restrictions. Some of us need freedom from the court system. It is overtaxing, overwhelming, and stressful, but our God is able to deliver.

God is here to set you free from whatever keeps you in bondage. We no longer have to live under the burden of the law. We can live under the authority and power of God.

> For God sent not his Son into the world to condemn the world; but that the world through him might be saved. (John 3:17)

DECLARATION

I declare that every scar will now become my star. It will be a reminder of who I am and Whose I am. I will walk in authority over ever satanic attack from the Enemy and cast down every lie that is spoken with against me. I declare that I will agree with God that I am a victor. I am a woman of power, grace, beauty, nobility, and strength walking in my true freedom.

PRAYER

Dear heavenly Father, I come before You surrendering my will for Your will. I loose the chains of bondage over my life today, and I speak freedom through the power and blood of Jesus Christ. I have the freedom to live, the freedom to love, the freedom to serve You and do Your will. I speak a new beginning in my heart and in my mind. I declare that my mind is transformed, and I break down every stronghold that has been set up in my thoughts. I speak that the liberty that comes from serving You will operate in my life. I will walk in Your favor and newness. I decree and declare that I am free. I have a strategy that will be revealed to me through Your Spirit so that I can continue to walk in Your will. In the matchless name of Jesus Christ, I pray. Amen.

CHAPTER 8

CAUGHT IN THE CROSS FIRE

Too many times when husbands and wives decide to divorce, they forget the most important people in this situation. We fail to understand that our children will have to decide whose side to take or not take, whom to believe or not believe, whom to trust or not trust.

As parents, no matter how we try to explain it, make sense of it or even make things normal, we can't. Divorce is as cold as death. It is an experience that shapes the thoughts, opinions, actions, and behaviors of our children leaving invisible, unforgettable scars. There are both negative and positive factors in every situation. The question is how can parents help produce healthy outcomes from devastating experiences?

The first thing that parents need to avoid is selfishness, thinking only about their pain, hurt, lives, and feelings. Now, this is not what every parent does, but most of them do.

Some parents do reach out to the children while trying to hold things together themselves. Trust me; I get it. I went through a depression that left me with barely enough energy to fight for myself. Hence, my reference to selfishness relates mainly to parents who continue to disrespect, dishonor, and abuse each other verbally and physically in front of their children. This is a devastating experience for children, and they get caught in the crossfire.

When a mother and father insult and degrade each other, they are actually running an ugly campaign to expose each other's negative traits in front of the children. You may be speaking the truth, blatant lies, or what the other parent believes. Whichever is the case, the children are influenced to choose one parent over the other. In the end, both parents lose because it is a heavy emotional burden for their children to carry.

THE SINS OF THE FATHER

I believe people can change, be healed, delivered, and set free. However, when people do not live in total freedom through the blood of Jesus Christ, they are capable of doing and becoming whatever their nature and fleshly desires entice them to become or do.

Some parents are aware of the unfavorable traits or habits of their mothers and fathers and vow never to be like them. Nonetheless, in an attempt not to be like their parents, ofttimes, they journey on a different path of destruction with the same familiar spirit of their parents. The circumstances may be different, but the end result is the same. The Adversary will not allow them to see the error of their ways.

For this reason, when we are raising our families in Christian homes, we must always be on high alert for generational curses. We must pray and break them to change the cycle in our lives, as well as our children's lives. As parents, we have a major responsibility to teach and instruct our children in a godly manner, the way Christ wants us to.

> As arrows are in the hand of a mighty man; so are children of the youth. (Psalm 127:4)

This Scripture lets us know that we are to point our children in the direction they should go. We should teach them what is right even when we think they don't want to hear it.

> Train up a child in the way he should go: and when he is old, he will not depart from it. (Proverbs 22:6)

If you are a parent, be encouraged. We are not perfect. We make mistakes, and we can only do the best that we can to set good examples for our children to live by. I am so glad that God understands when we are hurting and hears our cries when we are crying on our children's behalf.

TRAIN UP A CHILD

We are living in perilous times, and the days are evil. However, as long as we commit our ways to God, stay on our knees, and walk upright before Him, our children will one day remember what we instilled in them and be saved. Sometimes, just like the prodigal son, they may go their way, but we must hold on to the promises of God and watch them come to pass.

> *The first thing that parents need to avoid is selfishness.*

Every child is different and unique. If you separately interview seven children raised in the same household with the same mother and father about their childhood and upbringing, you may be amazed at the answers. The children could have done the same activities, gone to the same church, ate the same food, and gotten the same educational opportunities, but they will all have totally different perspectives on how things went down.

Ironically, parents who feel they did their best would hear some jaw-dropping answers because children are all different individuals. Perspective is a powerful thing; we can all see the same thing, but interpret it differently.

Some children may get second-hand information from another sibling, while other siblings may have actually witnessed the events. Some siblings are shielded all together, while others choose to dismiss what they know because they just can't handle it.

As parents, we have to be careful. We must take the time to pray for and with our children. Never ever be too proud to say you are sorry when you are wrong. Teach your children about the power of forgiveness and reconciliation, not only by your words but by your actions. It will bless their lives in the years to come.

My father hated when we mistreated each other as siblings but turned around and showed extra kindness to our friends (my daddy did not play that). There were nine children in my family – eight girls and one boy. My brother was the seventh child, and I was number eight. Of course, I was a little tomboy trying to hang with him and his friends; we would have a blast. But every now and then, he would sneak up on me and punch me in my arm as hard as he could. We called this giving each other a frog because if you could hit the person's arm very hard, it would make your shoulder feel and look like it would leap. I would do the same thing to him, but I was his little sister. He knew better than that!

He would make me sick! Some days, I couldn't stand him, but I loved him so much. How mad he made me determined if I was going to tell on him or not, so he could get a whipping.

THICKER THAN WATER

Children can be pulled in many different directions causing severe and unnecessary pain. Parents, wake up and grow up! Stop taking your anger out on other people. Stop destroying family relationships! I repeat: stop destroying family relationships.

Weddings, birthdays, the birth of grandchildren and even death are major occasions that should bring families together. Don't you want peace and happiness? Wouldn't you like to make a happy event worthwhile for your children without any negative vibes? If you are too immature, full of pride, hateful, and selfish to do so shame on you! One day, you will wish you had done things differently.

I pray and believe that you will think long and hard about your choices. Allow God to heal your heart. Start anew today. Do your part, and let God do the rest. I love you in Christ, and I believe in you to make the right choice.

IT'S NOT ABOUT YOU

Yes, it has been rough. It has been hard, and you can't stand your ex. I'm sure your ex probably can't stand you either, but guess what? It is not always about you; it's about the lives God has entrusted into your hands. Be very careful.

As I stated earlier, there will be events that parents will share because of their children. During the time that I was writing this book, my eldest daughter got married. The turmoil I experienced with her father made this occasion one of great concern to me. Up until this point, he did not want to be in the same room I was in, so I was not sure how things were going to turn out.

It was about seven years after our divorce. I had made many attempts to communicate and be cordial for our children's sake, but it was not what he wanted. However, I prayed, and I asked God to allow my daughter's wedding day to be peaceful and enjoyable. It was her special day. After all, it was neither about him nor me. It was about our precious little girl who had grown into a beautiful woman.

The praise report is that everything was lovely! He gave her away, and we were both very proud in spite of everything. God got the total victory and the glory. Our ability to be in the same room peacefully with our children was totally off the Richter scale; their hearts were full and excited. My son danced with his sister and broke out doing the James Brown. I kid you not! It was a great success.

My daughter blessed my heart and soul when she said she felt a new beginning of healing for our family. This happened when she saw her father and me standing at the door of the room where she had gotten prepared for her special day. That meant the world to me because I know that there is nothing too hard for God to do.

WHAT REALLY MATTERS

Thank God for every little victory He allows us to experience where we can see His powerful hand working. At times, I admit it was difficult to share the joys of my children's marriages and the birth of my grandchildren with my ex. I felt like it was unfair that he got to partake and enjoy the celebrations when he was not available or supportive through the growing pains of our children's lives. I felt he caused immense damage, and I was left to pick up the pieces of their broken hearts. I had to comfort and soothe the feelings of embarrassment, abandonment, and hurt. I was the one who encouraged them to keep the faith and trust in God.

It was a lot for me to carry, so I had to remain strong, be the responsible parent, and hold my peace. I had to remind myself that even though I may have been justified to feel as I did, I needed to thank God and be grateful that he did eventually start to show support.

He made himself available for those major events in our children's lives when he could have chosen not to. I know it was a blessing to my children, and it made a difference in their lives; that is what mattered above all else. Now, when I look back at where God has brought my children and me from and the healing that continues to take place, all I can say is *Thank You, Lord, for all You have done for us!*

Broken marriages that involve children create a variety of emotions. However, aim to respond to every situation in a manner that pleases God and gives your children the wisdom, as well as and the tools to help them win in life.

Our children also experience deep emotional trauma as a result of divorce. They have no control over the parents' decisions and that is stressful for any child caught in the crossfire. So parents let us mature and become the mothers and fathers God expects us to be. May we cover our children in prayer because prayer changes things.

I can honestly say that because of the demise of the marriage to my kid's father, I assumed that marriage was something that they would never want to experience. They witnessed the hurt and devastation of not just their parents, but two leaders in ministry who could not salvage their own home and marriage.

I thank God for the miracle that I have witnessed in my children's lives when my third daughter, Jada, got married. Her older sister Janay had words at the reception. She began to share with everyone how they were all the product of divorce and didn't think that marriage was what they ever wanted. She blessed me when she said that she thought about the fact that God is love and He is also a God of forgiveness and that marriage was simply a miracle. I thank God for continual healing, forgiveness and victory.

DECLARATION

I declare that I will be the parent God expects me to be. I will instruct my child(ren) to love and serve Him diligently. I will be an example of how to go through challenging times and remain faithful to God. I declare that I will not plant toxic seeds in their hearts because of my hurt and pain that may cause them to stumble. I will do my best to do it God's way.

PRAYER

Father, we thank You for our children. You have entrusted us to train and raise them up in the way that they should go. Give us wisdom, knowledge, and understanding to rear our children. We are not perfect parents, but we strive to do the best that we can. Show us how to entreat our children and minister to their needs individually. As they become adults may they acknowledge You in their ways, so You will direct their paths. We love and trust You Father. In Jesus' name. Amen.

CHAPTER

SEASONS

This book was written to encourage, inspire, and help others who have encountered life-changing experiences. The contents of it expose some personal issues associated with my journey. However, it was written with a pure heart and a prayerful spirit.

I want my children to read the contents and be proud of the message in the ministry God gave me. These messages were given to make others aware of Satan's devices, so they could arm themselves with the whole armor of God. Moreover, they can fight the good fight of faith through any challenging circumstances, be victorious, and declare freedom from bondage and satanic attacks.

My children mean the world to me. God has encouraged me to be an example to them even when things didn't look so good. I experienced feelings of hopelessness and defeat, but I had to hold on to God for my children. I am still holding on with gratitude for each of them.

I used to believe I was a late bloomer. Being one of the youngest, I would lean on my older siblings for words of comfort and wisdom. God has always had a plan for me, but it was not fully realized.

Eventually, I discovered I was not a late bloomer; rather, I bloomed in season. My season came upon me, and I wasn't aware of it because it didn't look like what I imagined it to be.

Through the power of God and His infallible Word, I had to declare what was not to be so. It was a bitter, cold season for me. It looked lifeless, broken, decapitated, and mangled. I felt sad, lonely, scared, embarrassed, depressed, angry, displaced, and without direction. I had to fight for survival on the inside to change what would manifest on the outside.

When we are going through our seasons, we have to trust God, become childlike, and see things from a whole new perspective. During the winter season, there's a risk catching pneumonia, being caught out in frigid temperatures, or being devastated by a snowstorm. When you change your perspective of a snowstorm, you will notice that when the sun begins to shine, everything around you starts to shimmer, catch the light, and sparkles like diamonds in the snow. Isn't it a consolation to know that even in the winter, God will surround you with His love, warmth, and comfort?

As children, we lived in the moment, made memories, and enjoyed every second. This is what God wants us to continue to do because life happens. So yes, there is an undesirable side to your season, but I declare that this day, you are a trailblazer. You will show others through the wisdom of God how to pull out spiritual gifts and tools from His Word, our road map. Your ability to stand through the storm and come out blessed, encouraged, and highly favored gives others the courage and faith to know that they too can survive.

I know what it's like to see and feel your life as you know it crumble to the ground. I know what it's like to feel vulnerable, exposed, abandoned, like a complete outcast. You find yourself searching for you, trying to find a new normal. Wow! What a heart-wrenching experience.

When you have to define yourself as a single person after being married, it is a literal shock to your being. Thus, it causes traumatic stress as you try to understand what went wrong, why, and what could have been done differently. Along with the sudden panic in your chest and lingering pain that stings as if you touched a hot stove, it leaves a lasting impression that overwhelms you. But thank God! As you truly seek His face through every challenging phase, you too can be restored by declaring victory and triumph.

Don't get caught in the trap of thinking about the mistakes that you've made along the way. Your emotional state of mind can cause you to become a stranger to yourself.

> *My season came upon me, and I wasn't aware of it.*

Through the power and authority of Jesus Christ, I command you to stop, pray, and begin anew. Today, right now, you can change and recover everything that the cankerworm and locust devoured – your peace, joy, happiness or whatever it may be. God will comfort you in ways that satisfy your soul and help you love Him even more through the toughest seasons of your life.

My eldest sister wrote a song years ago entitled, "Every Day Is a New Day." The lyrics ring so very true today.

> Every day is a new day.
> Every day a new walk,
> Every day with Jesus Christ
> We have a new experience.
> So, Lord, help me to take each day
> One day at a time.

> And help me to climb the mountains
> That seem so very high.
> Lord, I want each day
> To be a closer walk with You
> Because I want each day to be Yours.
> © Lady Patricia Wynn-Tau

COMFORT AND WARMTH

It is awesome to know that when we acknowledge the Creator every day, He can make all things new. He can cause the sun to shine in our winter seasons.

As a little girl growing up in Reno, Nevada, I was familiar with snowstorms during the wintertime. I associated that time of year with fun and perks. The amount of snowfall would determine our plans for fun.

We had a nice elevated driveway, which meant we would be sledding down the driveway, building a snowman, and making snow angels. We also made ice cream by adding milk and a little sugar. When it became so cold that our toes and fingers became numb, we knew it was time to go inside and be comforted by our parents' provisions. It was much like what the Father does for us when we need to be recharged.

I remember entering the house on those cold winter days. The first thing I felt was the warmth from the heat; it instantly thawed out our souls. We would take off our wet shoes and clothing and gather by the heater with a blanket.

Sometimes we would come together by the fireplace and enjoy a hot meal, hot chocolate or roasted marshmallows on the end of the wire hangers we dangled over the flames in the fireplace. God will comfort you in ways that satisfy your soul and help you love Him even more during the toughest seasons of your life.

Chapter 9 ■ Seasons

DECLARATION

I declare a season of victory over my life! I may not understand every circumstance or even know why I am facing certain challenges. However, God has never failed me. So I will trust Him in every season of my life.

PRAYER

Lord, I thank You for Your comfort in every season of my life whether things are good or bad. I know You are allowing me to develop for the greater things ahead. I thank You for every level of growth. I am grateful that You love me enough to cover, protect, and prepare me for the season that will bring me closer to You. In Jesus' name, I pray. Amen.

CHAPTER 10

LIVING TO SPEAK AND DECLARE

You are breathing, which indicates you are alive. Like me, you may have encountered challenging circumstances in your life. These challenges silently stole your belief that you could speak to your state of affairs declaring that change will take place for your victory.

> Death and life are in the power of the tongue: and they that love it shall eat the fruit thereof. (Proverbs 18:21)

By faith, speak life, love, freedom, health, peace, joy or whatever you need in your life. Pursue them and spiritually fight for what God has promised you. Declare it to be so and you will obtain what you ask for. Indulge and enjoy the outcome of your request.

WHAT ARE YOU LIVING FOR?

Are you living to just grow old and let life pass you by while you speak negative thoughts of defeat and doubt? Are you one of those people full of gifts, talents, and abilities who sits on the sidelines watching others fulfill their purpose while you procrastinate and let life pass you by?

Are you just talking about how and what you are going to do, while you grow old full of wasted passion and potential? Perhaps you allow fear to take over and rob you of opportunities. If you continue, you will never know the outcome of your greatness.

Maybe you are just too lazy to speak and declare greater things in your life. You have a cap on your success and refuse to do what it takes to get to the next level. Well, guess what? I declare that today is a brand new day, and you will speak life over every dead dream, purpose, and desire for your life. This can transpose into every area of your life.

CRYING IN SILENCE

I was so paralyzed at one point in life that my voice was literally stolen from me. I didn't realize it until I needed to fight for myself in an abusive relationship. The more I was yelled at and talked down to, the more scared I got to defend myself. I was afraid of disappointing my ex. I walked on eggshells trying not to be scolded for things I had no control over.

This went on for years until I shut down and so did my voice to speak and declare. To be honest, it was so severe that I look back now and think, *Wow, I didn't even believe I had the power to speak and declare change to my condition.* So I accepted what the Enemy presented to me. I was crying in silence.

Exercise and singing became new outlets for me to thrive. When I worked out, sometimes I would walk alone, complaining, crying, and asking God why I was going through this. However, all my complaining did was keep me from seeing results.

There was no faith being activated and absolutely no speaking and declaring. That was just what the Enemy wanted. He knows your hurts and wants to keep you so bound that you sink deeper and deeper into despair. However, when you start to change your posture, as well as your position and begin to walk in a new authority with faith-driven words of declaration, God can move on your behalf.

THE THIEF

There is a difference between being robbed and someone stealing from you. You see, when you are robbed, the robber confronts you face-to-face and demands what he or she wants from you. On the other hand, when someone steals from you, it is done a little bit at a time. You don't even realize that your valuables are gone until you try to look for them. How devastating! It's almost like being in a gunfight. When it is time to draw your weapon, you reach for it and you discover it is gone. Fear and panic overtake you, and you are left at the mercy of the attacker.

> *If you continue, you will never know the outcome of your greatness.*

The whole time you are left trying to figure out what happened to your power. You wonder what happened to your belief that you matter, have feelings, and are valuable. Over time, you shut down, remain silent, and become helpless because you are convinced that you are of no use.

My ex-husband's abusive words penetrated me as if my insides had been beaten with his fists. The aftermath of the words spoken was so hurtful I had to sleep it off. I had to take time to decompress and pray for healing to my vital organs and my mind.

NO WEAPON SHALL PROSPER

The negative words would play over and over again in my head; the only way to combat them was to speak and declare what the Word of

God had to say. His words were a weapon against me, but the Bible tells us that no weapons formed against us shall prosper. I had to stand on God's Word and not walk in the flesh.

> For the weapons of our warfare are not carnal, but mighty through God to the pulling down of strong holds; Casting down imaginations, and every high thing that exalteth itself against the knowledge of God, and bringing into captivity every thought to the obedience of Christ. (2 Corinthians 10:4–5)

We are fighting a spiritual battle that we can only win when we build up ourselves in our most holy faith, praying in the Holy Ghost. This will send protection our way and cover us in ways we do not understand.

Every demonic force that was working through my husband had to become subject to the Word of the Lord. My God had the power to destroy and cancel every destructive, negative word spoken against me.

I live to speak and declare who I am in God. I freely live in my purpose and walk in my destiny. It feels so good to know that I can do the will of God and see others freed and fulfilled in the process. Speak to your situation. Speak to your life, and walk in your purpose. Birth the vision God has given you through prayer, hard work, and determination. Watch God bring that thing to pass.

DECLARATION

I am a survivor; I am the head and not the tail. I can do all things through Christ who strengthens me. I am unstoppable. I have the favor of God on my life. All my needs are met, and I have more than enough. I am an overcomer through Him Who loved us. I declare that I will complete every task that is given to me by God to change lives and empower God's people. I am an atmosphere changer; I speak with power and authority. My God hears me when I pray and answers my prayers. I declare it to be so. In Jesus' name. Amen.

PRAYER

Lord Jesus, anoint my lips to speak when I need to speak and to declare what I need to declare with power and authority. I will not be afraid to silence the voice of the Enemy with Your powerful Word. I will speak life to every dead situation. I will guard my heart and mind through prayer and fasting. I am your daughter whom You created in your image, and I will represent you with the life that I live. In Jesus' name, I pray. Amen.

CHAPTER 11

MY SECRET

*S*hh… don't say a word. As a matter of fact, ponder your little secret and lock it away in your heart so deep that even you will pretend not to know what it is. We can go around all day every day keeping our true feelings and desires a secret from everyone else – or, at least, try to. We may fool some people, but we can't fool ourselves. Trust me; I've tried it.

In Chapter 11, I mentioned that the people closest to me (my friends and family) asked me if I was ready for a new relationship. At that time, I truly felt I was. I was confidently telling everyone, *Sure, of course, I am!* However, the end-result revealed the truth.

I was not mentally or emotionally ready. After experiencing another failed marriage, the secret I had buried in my heart began to come to the surface. This experience was the key that unlocked the very truth to my secret. I was holding on to a thread of hope to reconcile with the father of my children. *Oh my god! Am I crazy? What is my problem?* I thought to myself.

Even though our relationship became very toxic, I was lonely and afraid of starting over with someone new. I had no idea how the adjustment would work out. I felt as if it would be easier to settle back into what was familiar to me.

I would remind myself of the good times. It was good for a little girl bride who didn't realize she was in a dysfunctional and unhealthy relationship because her husband controlled it all. People can change and marriages can be reconciled, and I'm all for that. However, I don't condone abuse of any kind. Seek God for your true answer. Acknowledge God and let Him direct your path, so you can know His will for your life!

WHEN THE LIGHT COMES ON

Listen, the time will come when you can honestly get clarity. The light of the truth will come on as it did for me. My ex was having some health challenges, and I reached out. For a while, things were going well. There was cordial communication and plans to do some activities with our children. This made my heart feel hopeful in some way.

One day, a little phone conversation that was taken the wrong way caused the real person he always was to reemerge. He told me he was blessed to have me out of his life. That statement resolved the conflict within me. The little secret desire I had to be reconciled ended.

When he said those words, I listened and thought to myself, *Wow, he's blessed to have me out of his life*. I had done everything in my power to be kind, caring, and forgiving to this man in spite of the most unthinkable things he did to me. Yet, he called it a *blessing* that I was gone? This was totally incredible.

I wasn't perfect, but I know I was a good woman who did the best I could. Even though that statement was a punch in the gut, instead of

Chapter 11 ■ My Secret

allowing it to knock the wind out of me, I allowed God to intervene and speak to me through it. I will share that declaration with you later on in this chapter.

God is amazing! I prayed for direction. I prayed that He would show me once and for all what to do. That episode of cordial kindness between us was short-lived. It's not like I didn't try. But, I realized he still had several toxic emotions to deal with, which he refused to release and let go. I believe God gave me the answer I needed that day.

SEE IT FOR WHAT IT IS

I am reminded of the story of David and King Saul recorded in the book of 1 Samuel. David was anointed to be king, and God was with David; everybody knew it. The people cried out that Saul had slain his thousands and David his ten thousands. This caused Saul to become very jealous of David. Actually, he hated David because of the popularity he gained after he killed Goliath. This is powerful because even though Saul was still the king, God had already fired him from the job because of disobedience.

> *I was lonely and afraid of starting over with someone new.*

It's only a matter of time before we see the truth. Sometimes you can love someone to the point at which there is nothing you want more than to make them happy regardless of what they do. We continue to do the things we think may please them in hopes of seeing their hearts and minds changed for the better.

David loved Saul. As a young lad, he was sought after to play his harp for King Saul so the evil spirit that tormented him would depart. The king wanted to take David's life but again, God was with David.

One day, King Saul threw a javelin at David in an attempt to take his life. When David saw this, he ducked; it missed him. Yet, he continued to serve the king. Another time, King Saul threw his spear at David with the intention to pin him to the wall. David continued to serve. However, Saul attempted to murder David again, but this time, David knew he had to run away from Saul and everything he was familiar with.

Wake up! When you are in an abusive situation, you could lose your life, mind, self-esteem, value, and self-worth. Love yourself enough to seek help. There are some things you don't need to pray about; use common sense. Your life is valuable; there is only one you.

When will we see what we see, know what we know, accept it, and move on? The point I am trying to make is that sometimes we can see that a situation is detrimental; yet, we keep trying to make it work. We do so when God is trying to get us to see things for what they really are. He has something greater in store for us. We need to accept it, guard our hearts, and let God be God as He leads us. He is able to protect us while He deals with the King Sauls in our lives.

MY REVELATION

More than ever, I became aware that my little secret was keeping me from receiving what God wanted me to have in my life. I felt like I had to hold the secret in because I didn't want to look stupid or crazy to other people after the pain and hurt my ex put me through.

When people asked me if I thought that we would get back together, I would say things like, *Oh no! Are you kidding me? I would never take him back!* Secretly, I wanted to. Whew! That was my truth. As I tried to move forward, that little thread of hope would keep anyone I met from being exactly what I needed or wanted because I had not completely let go of the past.

Chapter 11 ■ My Secret

My God, I feel His freedom for you right now in the Holy Ghost. If you haven't let go of your past, you are blocking your future. God wants to restore you and give you so much more.

I remember the day I got off the phone with my ex. God began to give me a declaration of completion that freed me totally. It unmuted my heart and unlocked a secret that was blocking me from getting what God wanted me to receive.

I share the words God spoke to me below. Let your heart and mind agree as I did mine. Speak, decree, and declare these words. I don't know what your secret desires are but the ultimate question is if it is God's will and desire for your life. He gives us the freedom to decide what we want to do.

Not only do our fleshly desires delay our blessings, they also make our ways hard. Once we let go and let God, He will take over and move on our behalf.

I pray that today will be the beginning of a new start for you. You deserve to be happy and experience real love, joy, and peace. I pray that God's choice blessing for your life will overtake you. No more crying over the past because you are free through the power of Jesus.

He loves you with an everlasting love. After you have tried everything your way and failed, give Him a try and trust Him with all your heart. Even when it seems you cannot trace Him, just know that He is there. He will never leave or forsake you.

DECLARATION OF COMPLETION AND FREEDOM

Today, I receive my answer and give my inner being permission to move forward with my life! Hallelujah! I have no questions, no second-guessing, and absolutely no doubts in my mind. On this day, _____ anything I'm holding on to that is blocking my progress is officially released. I submit my will to the will of God. I give myself permission to live, love, laugh, breathe and hope again. I eradicate every familiar memory or thought that would cause me to waver and be indecisive about what is best for me. I will receive freedom in the power of Jesus Christ. I will walk in my newness. I will give my mind permission to be transformed by the Word and to be covered by the precious blood of Jesus. I will never again be bothered, haunted or wounded by words that cut, tear down or destroy me or my future. I will rejoice forever more and embrace my new beginning with new expectations. I will not compare the old things with my new ones. I will see my future through a new pair of eyes. These things I decree and declare shall be done in the matchless name of my Redeemer, Jesus Christ. Amen.

PRAYER

Thank You, Lord, for being the discerner of hearts and revealing all the hidden secrets of our hearts. We submit our ways to You. We consult You to guide us in every circumstance. Help us to pray Your will for our lives and walk therein. You know all about us and what is best for our lives. We receive every good and perfect thing that comes from You, which enables us to live more fulfilled lives. In Jesus' name, we pray. Amen.

CHAPTER 12

MY CHILDREN

JANAY

My firstborn, you are very intelligent, smart, and witty. You have brought so much joy to our lives. I pray God's choice blessings upon you. You're gifted and talented for a purpose and promise. Never cease to grow, learn and improve. Keep loving God and His infallible Word; it will never pass away. I love you with all my heart.

JASHE

My second oldest, we are so proud of you. Girl, you're amazing. You work hard to make things happen. You became a mother at a young age and have done an amazing job taking care of our first grandgirl, Ziia. She's always on point and beautiful with signature hairdos by her mommy. Keep God first in all that you do and never settle for less. I love you to life.

JADA

My third oldest, we can always count on you, Jada Jewel. You remind me of your grandma Rochelle – cleaning, cooking, and getting things done. You're smart as a whip, and we are so thankful for you. Your laugh is contagious; no one can duplicate it. It is a Jada original. You are a blessing to us all, and I know God has great things in store for you. I love you very much.

JERONE

Junior, my only born son, God blessed me with you. I remember the day I gave birth to you after having three girls. I felt so excited for you, son. Even while I was giving birth to you, I felt the strength of the Lord. To me, that's what you represent – strength. You can accomplish anything you put your heart and mind to do. Strive to be an exceptional black man. Represent God first; seek His face, and He will bless you in all that you do. Be accountable to the good men God places in your life. They can pour the wisdom of God into you and show you how to be a man of honor and integrity in every phase of your life. I love you so much, and I'm very proud that you are my son.

JAYA, A.K.A. NURSE ROSE

My baby girl, oh my goodness! This one here should win an academy award (LOL). Jaya, you have brought so much joy to our lives. You're so full of love, life, energy, and drama! Girl, it's true what they say. You babies know how to get housework done without really doing it – okay, sometimes. Most times I must put my foot down; however, you are a good girl who loves God with all your heart. You are gifted and talented. You always let it be known that you will be a successful millionaire who you will pay all Mommy's bills and buy her a house

Chapter 12 ■ My Children

and a car (LOL). You are very caring and thoughtful, also as sweet as can be. I constantly receive good reports from teachers who are always excited about how pleasant you are while keeping your grades up. Sweetheart, Mommy loves you and is so blessed to have you as a daughter. You are an angel, and I love you so much. Stay sweet.

ZIIA

You are the sweetest little baby girl, and we all love you to pieces. You are so special to us all. You're growing every day, and you are so smart learning your alphabets, numbers, colors, words, and everything that prepares you to be the smartest in your class. I am so blessed to be able to see you grow. You love God and love to clap and sing His praises. You are a gift to us all. Your mama, as you call her, keeps you camera ready, and you don't mind posing for the camera (LOL). I pray that you always keep Jesus in your heart. Lola – or as you always call me, Mom (because you hear everybody else call me that) –wants you to know I love you so much. We are blessed to have you, sweet pea!

> *My prayer for my children is that they will have healthy relationships.*

LUIS, JR. A.K.A. LJ

My first grandson, I am just tickled pink. Even as a baby, you have the most pleasant spirit ever. Your laughter and happiness are just so contagious. I love you with all my heart, and I pray that you grow up to be the young man God is calling you to be, a young man who loves Him with all your heart. You are growing so fast, and I enjoy how you are giving your mother the treatment that she gave me staying up all night – just kidding. I am very happy to have such a handsome grandbaby.

[Luis Antonio Anguiano is the newest addition in my family bouquet. I love him so much and I am so proud. Rio Vista, CA in December 2018. Photographer Jacqueline Ojeda.]

PRAYER

My prayer for my children is that they will have healthy, non-toxic or abusive relationships. I pray that the poisonous residue from the traumatic experiences of the past will be cursed and rebuked from your lives and the generations to come. May they take the devastating experience of divorce and use it as a stepping-stone to be better. You don't have to be a victim of divorce; you can hold your families together. It is not going to be easy, but you can do it with the help of the Lord. Continue to pray without ceasing and be wise people who build your homes. I pray for my son to be a man of integrity and patience loving God and his wife-to-be. I also pray that he covers and protects my children and grandchildren. In Jesus' name. Amen. You are all great children, and I am very glad that God gave you to me.

Love,
Your mother

Chapter 12 ■ My Children

[L-r Jerone, Jada, Janay, Sharon, Jaya, Ziia and Jashe. A picture I wanted to take before the close of the year to represent us moving forward and being a strong unit together. Fairfield, CA in December 2015. Photographer Eric Marshall.]

[This picture of us represents their different personalities. They are all very unique and so much fun.]

OTHER WORKS BY THE AUTHOR

ACKNOWLEDGMENTS

To my children, I love all of you very much. I am grateful for every milestone, holiday, birthday, graduation, wedding, and birth of a grandchild I have shared with you. Each event has made me a wealthy woman, and I have cherished every moment. I thank God for His goodness and for helping me to provide for you all even when it seemed as if things were falling apart.

To my dad Carlton Anderson, my mother Rochelle Anderson, my father the late Rev. W. J. Wynn, my baby sister who has passed on, Ms. Rachel Christine Wynn, all my siblings, my brothers-in-law, and sisters-in-law. I love you all and thank you for your love, support, and prayers.

To my writing mentor and author, Mrs. Janie P. Bess, thank you for all your encouragement, love, and support.

To my daughter, Mrs. Janay Anguiano, thank you for your love and support; you type faster than lightning.

To Ms. Vanessa Miller, thank you for helping me to get the ball rolling.

To Ms. Jennifer Howard, thank you so much for helping me with editing. You were a true lifesaver.

To author Lady Vicki Kemp, thank you for mentoring me and giving me great ideas and useful information. I am so grateful for your selflessness. You are my sister and I love you.

To Mr. Leon Johnson, thank you for believing in me and encouraging me to go the extra mile.

ABOUT THE AUTHOR

[For this photo and cover photos. 2019. Photographed by Marcus McCauley Sessions. Make-up by Vadia Rhodes]

Sharon R. Wynn is an author, recording artist, songwriter, inspirational speaker and anointed woman of God. Born in Reno, Nevada to the late Pastor W. J. Wynn and Rochelle Wynn-Anderson, she is the eighth of nine children.

The proud mother of five beautiful children and two lovely grandchildren, Lady Wynn owns Little Arrows childcare, the goal of which is to point children towards success through early childhood learning and development. As the founder of New Beginnings Women's Empowerment Groups she encourages, celebrates and supports women – from all walks of life – who have encountered life's hardships. Lady Wynn also ministers to women in transitional homes who seek to change their lives as she imparts hope and new direction through the Word of God.

Lady Wynn accepted the call to ministry at the age of ten and has worked in different capacities, including co-pastoring for several years. She is perfectly designed to fulfill a mandate to write, speak and sing with a message of hope to reach those who've lost hope. Her prayer is that through her ministry, lives will be changed, renewed and restored.

AUTHOR CONTACT

www.ladywynn.com

info@ladywynn.com

www.ingramcontent.com/pod-product-compliance
Lightning Source LLC
LaVergne TN
LVHW052255070426
835507LV00035B/2936